SCHOOL CHOICE

The MIT Press Essential Knowledge Series

SCHOOL CHOICE

DAVID R. GARCIA

The MIT Press | Cambridge, Massachusetts | London, England

This book was set in Chaparral Pro by Toppan Best-set Premedia Limited. Printed and bound in the United States of America.

Library of Congress Cataloging-in-Publication Data

Names: Garcia, David R., author.
Title: School choice / David R Garcia.
Description: Cambridge, MA : The MIT Press, 2018. | Series: The MIT Press essential knowledge series | Includes bibliographical references and index.
Identifiers: LCCN 2018010195 | ISBN 9780262535908 (pbk. : alk. paper)
Subjects: LCSH: School choice—United States. | Education and state—United States
Classification: LCC LB1027.9 .G37 2018 | DDC 379.1/110973—dc23 LC record available at https://lccn.loc.gov/2018010195

10 9 8 7 6 5 4 3 2 1

CONTENTS

SERIES FOREWORD

The MIT Press Essential Knowledge series offers accessible, concise, beautifully produced pocket-size books on topics of current interest. Written by leading thinkers, the books in this series deliver expert overviews of subjects that range from the cultural and the historical to the scientific and the technical.

In today's era of instant information gratification, we have ready access to opinions, rationalizations, and superficial descriptions. Much harder to come by is the foundational knowledge that informs a principled understanding of the world. Essential Knowledge books fill that need. Synthesizing specialized subject matter for nonspecialists and engaging critical topics through fundamentals, each of these compact volumes offers readers a point of access to complex ideas.

Bruce Tidor
Professor of Biological Engineering and Computer Science
Massachusetts Institute of Technology

A BRIEF HISTORY OF
SCHOOL CHOICE

At first blush, school choice may appear noncontroversial. In fact, some may even consider it a humdrum topic. Most parents and other citizens may have put little thought into the decision of which schools students attend. Nevertheless, school choice is one of the most controversial public policy issues of our time. What makes school choice controversial is the core question: Who has the authority to determine which schools students can attend? Should the decision be determined by elected officials acting on behalf of their community and administered through government-controlled school systems? Or should parents be allowed to make school choice decisions based on individual interests? The answers to these questions have shaped education policy for the past sixty years and will continue to be a central issue for years to come. The future direction of school choice policies will have extensive implications that alter the organization and delivery of public education and influence educational and societal outcomes for all students.

This book offers a broad and accessible discussion of school choice that is written for a general audience. I focus on the major issues and arguments typically encountered in the public discourse on school choice, that is, how school choice is discussed in media accounts and in education policy settings. The discussion centers on the United States because of its long history with school choice and influential role in education policy. Nevertheless, I also address major international school choice policies. My goal is to equip readers with a working knowledge of school choice so they can contribute to policy discussions in their local setting.

This book is organized into four chapters. Chapter 1 introduces the major school choice policies. Chapter 2 presents a discussion of the major arguments that support school choice policies along with the respective counterarguments. Chapter 3 reviews the research on school choice policies. Finally, chapter 4 offers a preview of how school choice policies are likely to evolve in the future.

I address the general trends associated with school choice. Thus, it is possible that readers may be able to find individual examples in their local setting or specific research that contradicts the contents of this book. But to the extent that my treatment of school choice is an accurate reflection of the key findings and themes in the field and under discussion in policymaking settings, these contradictory examples will be the exception, not the rule.

This chapter is organized chronologically, with the most recent school choice proposals presented last. It examines multiple types of school choice: home schooling, private schools, freedom-of-choice plans, magnet schools, charter schools, vouchers, and education savings accounts. In addition to a general overview of school choice policies, it introduces common themes: that school choice policies are inextricably tied to school desegregation efforts and that these policies influence the role and responsibilities of individuals versus government as they pertain to one of the most fundamental requirements of government: educating its citizenry. These themes, which recur throughout the book, define the contours of school choice debates and will reoccur in future policy discussions.

Home Schooling

For most of American history, student assignment to public schools was not a contentious policy issue. In fact, it was hardly a policy issue at all. In the earliest years of the United States, students who attended school did so in the schoolhouse in their town. The one-room schoolhouse was a common feature of American towns from the colonial days through the agrarian period. Local communities also began to incorporate taxing authorities to pay for school expenses.

As the Industrial Revolution forced migration from rural communities to America's urban centers, public schools continued to be constructed based on population growth and local demand. As families established new neighborhoods, public schools were constructed to accommodate the growing student population living in the immediate area, and districts created policies to enforce school attendance boundaries to manage operations and avoid overcrowding. Even in urban areas, the preponderance of students attended the neighborhood public school located closest to their home.

Other schooling alternatives, such as home schooling and private schools, have existed alongside public schools since the inception of public education in the United States. For example, in areas where there was no public school available, education, when conducted, occurred at home. Even when public schools became available in most areas, some parents preferred to home-school their children for several reasons, including to impart a particular learning method, have more influence over the socialization of their children, and provide religious education alongside academic preparation. The need to establish home schooling as a legally recognized school option arose as a result of compulsory education laws that required parents to enroll their children in a public school until their child reached a minimum age, often between sixteen and eighteen years old. Compulsory education laws date back to the mid-1600s, and by 1918, all states had passed a compulsory education law that remains in effect (Katz 1976). Today, home school parents assume responsibility for the education of their student and release the state of such responsibility. Home schooling requirements in the United States vary by state (Prothero 2018). In most states, home schooling instruction does not have to be conducted by someone with a teaching certificate, and in some states, home schooling students are required to take state-mandated assessments. In 2012, 1.8 million US students (3.4 percent of all US students) were home-schooled (National Center for Education Statistics 2015, table 206.10). The primary thrust of contemporary public policy efforts for home-schooled students and parents is creating networks to connect with each other and gaining access to educational materials.

Private Schools

Private schools are a common and long-standing feature of American education. There are many types of private schools, including independent schools. In general, private schools are autonomous institutions, do not receive public funding, and are not required to follow many state laws that pertain to public schools. They remain in operation through tuition, fees, charitable donations or an endowment. Parents of private school students pay for their tuition. As taxpayers, these parents also pay all applicable taxes to support public schools, even though their students do not attend a public school.

In the 2013–14 academic year, 33,619 private schools (25 percent of all US schools) enrolled 5.4 million students 11 percent of all US students) in kindergarten through twelfth grade ((http://www.capenet.org/facts.html). Sixty-seven percent of private schools are affiliated with a religion, and religious private schools enrolled 78 percent of the total private school population (National Center for Education Statistics 2017a). On average, private schools are smaller than traditional public schools, enrolling fewer students on individual campuses. They also enroll a higher percentage of white students and a lower percentage of minority students than traditional public schools do (Southern Education Foundation 2016). Finally, families with students attending private schools are wealthier on average than public school families (Reardon and Yun 2002).

While many of the school choice policies discussed in this book are intended to allow students to attend private schools using public funds, by and large, these policies have not been advanced by private schools themselves.

In fact, the private school response to vouchers is mixed. Some private school associations, such as the National Catholic Education Association, favor vouchers (https://www.ncea.org), while support for vouchers among other religious groups remains a contested issue (Religious Action Center of Reform Judaism 2017). And some private schools view school choice policies with skepticism out of a concern that accepting public funds will subject them to state regulations and jeopardize their standing as autonomous institutions.

Historically, enrolling in private schools or home-schooling students were not considered an expression of school choice in the same manner that they are viewed today. When students attended a schooling alternative instead of the local public schools, it was regarded as an individual parental preference. Education policies related to private schools and home schooling focused on establishing both types of schooling as legitimate, autonomous options, independent of the public school system and exempt from compulsory public school attendance requirements. Parents who sent their children to parochial schools or home-schooled their children did so on their own accord, paying tuition and other educational expenses through private funds. Also, there were few public policies that diverted resources away from the public school system when students availed themselves of home schooling or private school alternatives. There were few public policy debates about the use of public funds for students to attend private schools.

The arrangement where most students attended the neighborhood public school, with attendance boundaries based on geographic proximity, continued largely unaltered until the 1950s. For our purpose, student attendance at the neighborhood public schools has a couple of important implications. First, the racial/ethnic composition of students attending public schools mirrored the racial/ethnic composition of the neighborhoods in which the schools were located. Second, school choice was not an education policy issue. Student attendance in a non–public school was not used to accomplish other policy goals, such as education reform.

Freedom-of-Choice Plans and School Attendance Policies

The earliest references to school choice policies emerged in response to *Brown v. Board of Education*, the 1954 landmark case to desegregate American public schools. Although *Brown* is not commonly associated with the contemporary public discussion about school choice, it was the genesis of school choice as a public policy mechanism. *Brown* dictated that school districts desegregate public schools "with all deliberate speed" (Brown v. Board of Education 1955). School attendance boundaries at the time of the decision, however, were largely based on geographic proximity. Black and white students lived in different neighborhoods and therefore attended different schools. The desegregation of US public schools would require a fundamental change in the historical arrangement where students attended local neighborhood schools. In other words, given the tight geographic connection between schools and neighborhoods, desegregation meant that at some level, either white or black students (or both) would need to attend a school outside their neighborhood and farther away from their neighborhood public school. Breaking the geographic connection between students and the neighborhood school would prove to be a significant challenge to desegregation efforts, leading to considerable strife and discontent with public school attendance policies.

In response to *Brown*, many southern school districts eliminated laws mandating segregated schools for black and white students. They established freedom-of-choice plans that afforded students the right to attend any school in their school district of residence, regardless of race. Schools were prohibited from denying admission to students except in the case of overcrowding or other extraordinary conditions. In this way, students could choose to attend any school, as school districts intended to desegregate schools by choice. Southern school districts argued that freedom-of-choice plans met the mandate of *Brown* because "racial separation under *free* choice can only result

Breaking the geographic connection between students and the neighborhood school would prove to be a significant challenge to desegregation efforts, leading to considerable strife and discontent with public school attendance policies.

from the individual's school selection. The state will not force him to attend the school nearest his home, and under a properly administered plan, there is no state involvement in the pupil's selection" (Brown 1968, 459).

Freedom-of-choice plans ended de jure segregation, or the legal requirements that schools be segregated by race, but they did not end de facto segregation. Schools remained effectively divided by race. Due to the intense social pressures associated with attending integrated schools, very few white students chose to attend black schools and very few black students chose to attend white schools. The conclusion from freedom-of-choice plans was that simply affording the opportunity to choose was an insufficient method to desegregate schools.

The constitutionality of freedom-of-choice plans was litigated until 1968, when the U.S. Supreme Court ruled such plans as unconstitutional (Green v. County School Board of New Kent County 1968). Ultimately the courts concluded that school districts not only had the duty to eliminate segregation policies but they must also take affirmative steps to desegregate public schools. By the mid-1970s, school districts had ended freedom-of-choice plans. In response, school districts implemented mandatory student attendance and busing policies. Mandatory attendance policies dictated student assignments to specific schools in an effort to achieve a racial balance. Busing policies required that students be transported out of their neighborhood to a neighborhood and school composed of people and students belonging to another racial group. Both policies were unpopular with parents. Mandatory student attendance policies disregarded parental preference with respect to school assignments, and busing policies required some students to travel great distances to attend a desegregated school rather than attending the nearest neighborhood school.

The hostility toward mandatory student attendance and busing policies aroused the tension between parental choice and court mandates. Parents felt that they had the right to choose the school that their student attended. School boards, bound by court mandates to implement the remedies required by *Brown*, exerted their authority to determine student attendance requirements. It was during this period of American public education that the idea of school choice took hold as a public policy issue.

Through a combination of school district policy and court orders, school districts turned to school choice as a key policy driver to desegregate schools. One version, controlled school choice, combined parental preference and school district control to regulate student schooling assignments. Controlled school choice was intended to incorporate parental preference in school assignments and temper opposition to mandatory school attendance and busing policies while still complying with *Brown* (Fava 1991). In contrast to freedom-of-choice plans, controlled choice plans did not allow unfettered parental choice to determine student placement in schools. Rather, parents indicated their school choices in priority order. School districts then assigned students to individual schools to meet specific racial quotas to achieve student body compositions that were proportional to the demographics of the local community. Controlled-choice plans were intended to allow parents to prioritize their school choices based on the needs and best interests of their child.

Despite taking parental preferences into consideration in the assignment of students to schools, controlled-choice plans were also unpopular. When students were not assigned to their top school choice, they were often required to travel considerable distances to attend schools located far from their neighborhoods. White families were particularly dissatisfied with controlled-choice plans, forced school attendance boundaries, and busing. They were also those in the best economic position to move their residence so that their students could attend the schools that their parents preferred. Thus, white families exited urban neighborhoods and schools in large numbers to live and attend schools in suburban areas. The mass exodus of white students from central cities to the suburbs that occurred beginning in the 1960s is known as *white flight*. Its practical result was a return to segregated schooling conditions because many minority students remained concentrated in urban schools.

Magnet Schools

School districts turned to other voluntary school choice policies, particularly magnet schools, to further their desegregation efforts and attract white students back to urban schools. Magnet schools, introduced in the early 1970s, began as alternative schooling options supported by financial assistance from the federal government. These alternative schools were, and remain, popular with parents, attracting students from diverse racial groups and social classes. They are called "magnets" for their ability to attract a diverse student body.

Magnet schools are public schools designed around specialized curricula or theme-based programs, such as science and math or the arts, or they may offer an advanced curriculum, such as a concentration of honors courses or an International Baccalaureate program. Magnet schools often are regarded as flagship schools in a local school district and develop reputations as elite public schools. They offer an educational experience that is distinct from the traditional public schools in a local community in order to attract students, and parents, who share a similar academic interest. To promote desegregation, magnet schools are often located in minority neighborhoods in order to attract students from outside the immediate neighborhood, specifically white students living in suburban neighborhoods. The number of magnet schools has remained steady for the past decade, constituting approximately 3 percent of all public schools (National Center for Education Statistics 2015, table 216.20). Expensive to operate, these schools are a common target for elimination or reduction when budget cuts are looming.

With respect to school choice, the purpose and role of magnet schools have evolved as education policies have moved toward market-driven school choice programs and away from race-based admissions policies. While diversity was once a pillar of magnet schools, they are no longer just tools to desegregate schools in some school districts. Magnet schools are often regarded as another school choice option available within the public school system to increase student enrollment.

School Vouchers

Milton Friedman, a University of Chicago economist, proposed universal school vouchers in 1955 in an article, "The Role of Government in Education." His universal voucher proposal involved giving parents vouchers redeemable at the school of their choice, public or private. The value of the voucher would be determined by the amount of money allocated per pupil by the state for students to attend public schools so that voucher programs would not constitute an additional cost to the state above the amount allotted for public education. Parents could also subsidize the voucher to purchase additional educational services. The precedent for Friedman's idea was the GI Bill, a widely used program that provided qualified veterans with a specified amount of money they could use for payment at the higher education institution of their choice, public or private, as long as the postsecondary institution met minimum requirements set by the federal government.

A couple of key details of Friedman's universal voucher proposal warrant mention because they became relevant in later school choice policies that built on the initial universal voucher proposal, such as education savings accounts. First, Friedman proposed that vouchers would be redeemable for educational services provided by educational institutions. The vouchers themselves did not have any cash value. Once redeemed by the parent at the chosen educational provider, the government provided payment to the provider for educational services. Second, Friedman's proposal expanded the selection of educational providers that could receive public funds well beyond public schools. He proposed that private enterprises, including for-profit organizations and private schools, could receive public funds to provide educational services so long as they meet the minimum requirements established by the government. Private schools were the most common nonpublic schooling alternatives at the time of Friedman's proposal, and most private schools had a religious affiliation. Thus, vouchers proposed the direct payment of public money by the government to religious schools.

Some broader implications of Friedman's universal voucher proposal continue to resonate in current public policy discussions. First, Friedman shifted the responsibility for education away from government institutions to individual families. This fundamental shift from government to families would later lead to viewing parents as educational consumers and government as one of many educational providers. To discern the consequences of this shift, it is important to understand the concept of education as a public good and how that concept is implemented in the establishment and operation of public schools. The role of government in education is justified because public education is regarded as a public good, that is, there is a collective benefit to an educated citizenry. In other words, on some level, all of society benefits from students getting an education, not just the student or the family themselves. This view of education as a public good is reflected by mandatory public education requirements in state constitutions that interpret state governments as responsible to fund and operate public schools for all students in a state. Before school choice policies became prominent, the primary role for parents was to ensure that their children attended school, a requirement that was codified by compulsory attendance laws. Little to no public policy

This fundamental shift from government to families would later lead to viewing parents as educational consumers and government as one of many educational providers.

attention was directed toward empowering parents to shop for schools or for the state to provide parents with multiple schooling alternatives and sufficient information to make school choice decisions.

Friedman was a free-market economist, however, and he applied the principles of market forces and limited governmental intervention to public services and institutions, including education. It follows, then, that Friedman would interpret the role of the individual broadly while curtailing governmental action. In support of his universal voucher proposal, he argued,

> In what follows, I shall assume a society that takes freedom of the individual, or more realistically the family, as its ultimate objective, and seeks to further this objective by relying primarily on voluntary exchange among individuals for the organization of economic activity. In such a free private enterprise exchange economy, government's primary role is to preserve the rules of the game by enforcing contracts, preventing coercion, and keeping markets free. (Friedman 1955, 23)

This perspective defined education as a private good, similar to other commodities bought and sold on the open market. In order for Friedman's universal voucher proposal to achieve the improved efficiency in education service delivery that he projected, there must be an education marketplace and parents must act like consumers, seeking to get the most benefits possible for their students through vouchers as a form of currency. Schools are then to act like private enterprises, or businesses, to attract and retain students.

Second, the expressed purpose of vouchers was to expand educational choices in order to infuse competition into education. Friedman targeted public schools because they were monopolized by state governments, and he argued that government monopolies and the bureaucracies that they engendered were inefficient. By way of context, nearly all public schools were funded and governed by state governments at the time of Friedman's proposal.

State governments came to control public education because the US Constitution does not grant the federal government authority over education. This authority was left to the states, and every state constitution contains mechanisms for provisions under which state governments are required to provide public education. In turn, many states vested the day-to-day management of public schools in locally elected school boards. This localized structure of education is unique compared to many other countries, where the federal government is charged with providing public education and schools are governed at the national level. Compared to countries with national education structures, many more decisions are made at the local level in the US public education system.

The core of Friedman's universal voucher proposal is to improve the delivery of services through choice and competition. For this reason, he intentionally opened up the pool of possible education providers to private enterprises outside the public school system, which, he argued, could more efficiently meet consumer demand for education than could government-run institutions. Friedman reasoned that universal vouchers would result in

> a sizable reduction in the direct activities of government, yet a great widening in the educational opportunities open to our children. They would bring a healthy increase in the variety of educational institutions available and in competition among them. Private initiative and enterprise would quicken the pace of progress in this area as it has in so many others. Government would serve its proper function of improving the operation of the invisible hand without substituting the dead hand of bureaucracy. (Friedman 1955, 144)

Third, vouchers proposed a fundamental shift in the role of government in public education. Friedman envisioned a much narrower governmental role in public education than had been the established practice up to that point in time. Vouchers changed the role of government from funding and providing education to funding and approving educational providers. The state was charged with "assuring that the schools met certain minimum standards such as the inclusion of a minimum common content in their programs, much as it now inspects restaurants to assure that they maintain minimum sanitary standards" (Friedman 1955, 125). In other words, state government would still fund education, but it was no longer the primary entity responsible for providing public education. Rather, this responsibility could be filled by many other institutions, organizations, or enterprises as long as these institutions met governmentally approved minimal standards.

At the time Friedman's universal voucher proposal was published, his idea was regarded as more academic than as a practical education policy alternative. Limiting the government's role was a radical idea because it ran counter to the day-to-day realities of most Americans. Government was the exclusive institution responsible for funding and operating public schools, and public funds were rarely diverted to other school choice alternatives. In addition, vouchers were considered unconstitutional because they violated laws that required the separation of church and state. Friedman's universal voucher proposal provides for direct payment by government to religious schools. The establishment clause of the First Amendment to the US

Constitution, however, prohibits the government from favoring a state-sponsored church through direct or indirect means, such as funding. Government is permitted to assist churches as long as the assistance is secular in nature and does not promote or inhibit a specific religion. The legal status of vouchers has been addressed by US courts since Friedman's proposal, a topic that is discussed in more detail later in this chapter.

Of the many counterarguments to Friedman's universal voucher proposal put forth by critics, three remain relevant to the current public policy discussion on vouchers and will likely remain relevant in the future. First, critics point out that history indicates that unregulated school choice policies, such as universal vouchers, segregate students along racial/ethnic lines and stratify students by socioeconomic class. The impact of school choice policies on segregation is addressed in chapter 3, along with the other empirical research on school choice.

Second, critics argue that universal vouchers exacerbate educational inequities. One reason is that vouchers are often an unrealistic school choice for many low-income students because of the full costs associated with attending a private school. Wealthier families are in the best position to take advantage of vouchers because they can pay for the additional costs associated with attending a private school, such as tuition that is above and beyond the value of a voucher. For the 2011–12 academic year, the average private school tuition was $13,640 (Council for American Private Education 2017), but the amount that would be available in a school voucher was $4,922, based on the average state-level funding allotment per pupil (US Census Bureau 2015). While some private schools offer need-based scholarships, wealthier parents by and large are in a more advantaged position to afford the full costs associated with attending a private school, including indirect costs such as transportation, books, and uniforms.

Furthermore, critics argue that under a universal program, there are no policy mechanisms to ameliorate educational inequities because markets are inherently inequitable. If the educational marketplace functions like the marketplace for other goods and services, one can expect higher- and lower-quality school options as a matter of course, depending on what communities can afford. One goal of US education policy is to eliminate educational inequities based on differences in local community wealth. A common goal among school choice proponents and opponents alike is that a student's zip code, where zip codes indicate a student's neighborhood of residence, should not determine access to a quality education.

Third, critics argue that education is a more complex good than other consumer products. The purpose of many consumer products is rather clear, and consumers are able to judge the quality of the product to meet the intended purposes and make the decision to purchase

A common goal among school choice proponents and opponents alike is that a student's zip code, where zip codes indicate a student's neighborhood of residence, should not determine access to a quality education.

(or repurchase) the product with sufficient time to generate the competitive forces necessary to create efficient markets.

In contrast, education is a complex consumer good. Its intended purposes are not clear or consistent across individual parents. Is the purpose of education to forge functional citizens? Teach basic academic skills such as reading, writing, and mathematics? Or instill values, even religious ones? Historically, the purposes of education were the content of public debate by elected school boards and enacted through public policies. Friedman's proposal shifted this responsibility to the family level, meaning that individual parents were encouraged to determine these purposes for themselves and select schools accordingly. Thus, what one parent may seek from a school on behalf of his or her child could be distinctly different from the educational preferences of another parent, assuming that both sets of parents are able to formulate their educational preferences well enough to make an informed decision.

Also, educational outcomes can be ambiguous and are often delayed. How are parents to judge if schools are meeting their specific educational purposes, even with something as noncontroversial as learning to read? Should parents place importance on standardized test scores or student demonstrations of reading ability, such as reading a recipe or a full-length book? Furthermore, how are parents to judge if their student is reading at grade level and learning the key foundational skills needed to remain on grade level in future years? Finally, how often should parents seek demonstrations of student learning? Weekly? Monthly? Or should they wait until the end of the school year?

School choice advocates recognize the importance of accurate, timely, and understandable information to parents in order to make informed school choice decisions. In an effort to equip parents with quality information, states publish school report cards that summarize key school programmatic information and academic performance results in a manner that allows comparisons across schools. The academic performance results include outcomes by school, such as standardized test scores, dropout rates, and graduation rates. School report cards may also include programmatic information, such as school uniform policies and before- and after-school offerings.

While providing information to parents, school report cards are not intended to establish common educational purposes across individual families. The factors by which parents choose schools for their children are still based on individual prerogatives and preferences. Parents choose schools based on any educational and noneducational purposes they see fit for their child. In addition, one key practical question in research on school choice is the extent to which school report cards factor into school choice decisions compared to the influence of informal information sources, such as word-of-mouth and private websites that include school-related information and parent ratings.

Despite considerable academic and public policy attention, vouchers have been implemented on only a limited scale and targeted toward low-income students, special education students, students attending low-performing schools, or rural students with no access to a public school. As of 2017, fourteen states and the District of Columbia offer voucher programs, and every program is targeted toward one of the student groups noted. There are no statewide, universal, market-based voucher programs in the manner that Friedman envisioned. One reason is that universal voucher programs have been unpopular with voters. Vouchers have been placed on the ballot in several states and have failed to garner voter approval.

The two most notable school voucher programs are located in Milwaukee and Washington, DC. Implemented in 1989, the Milwaukee voucher program was the first such program. The Washington, DC, voucher program began in 2004 and is often cited because it was the first federally funded program. Both programs have been the focus of considerable research, and much of what we know about the potential operation and outcomes of voucher programs stems from research in these two cities. Internationally, Chile's large-scale voucher program has also been the source of considerable research. The research outcomes of Chile's voucher program are addressed in more detail in chapter 3.

The legal arguments surrounding vouchers have centered on the payment of public funds to religious schools. While vouchers are made available to many private institutions, including private sectarian schools, opponents argue that the vast majority of non–public schools are religious schools, effectively directing public money to religious purposes. More recent iterations of school choice proposals, such as education savings accounts, circumvent the constitutional obstacles associated with vouchers by providing direct payment to parents to purchase educational services rather than providing parents a voucher to be reimbursed by the government.

In 2002, however, the US Supreme Court in *Zelman v. Simmons-Harris* upheld a voucher program in Ohio ruling that it did not violate the establishment clause despite allocating public funds for private religious schools. The voucher program, targeted to all students residing in severely underperforming school districts, distributed aid based on financial need, and public schools were eligible to participate in the program. Given these facts, the Court concluded,

> In sum, the Ohio program is entirely neutral with respect to religion. It provides benefits directly to

a wide spectrum of individuals, defined only by financial need and residence in a particular school district. It permits such individuals to exercise genuine choice among options public and private, secular and religious. The program is therefore a program of true private choice. In keeping with an unbroken line of decisions rejecting challenges to similar programs, we hold that the program does not offend the Establishment Clause. (Zelman v. Simmons-Harris 2002, 2473)

There are two important implications from *Zelman* for this discussion of school choice. First, the role of parental choice was a major factor in the Court's decision. The Court paid careful attention to verify the existence of parental choice in the voucher program and was careful to protect parents' rights to choose in its reasoning. In essence, the Court found that vouchers did not, in and of themselves, promote religion, but they did promote parental choice. This conclusion is important because parental choice continues to play an important role in the structure of school choice programs and how they are promoted to the public. Second, *Zelman* did not address the constitutionality of vouchers in thirty-seven states, all with a Blaine amendment, which expressly prohibits state governments from funding religious schools with public money (Institute for Justice 2017). Blaine amendments are generally more restrictive than the establishment clause, and *Zelman* does not compel states with a Blaine amendment to accept a voucher program that includes religious schools (Lantta 2004). Therefore, since *Zelman*, school choice advocates have developed school choice programs, such as education savings accounts, that could circumvent Blaine amendments.

Charter Schools

In 1988, Albert Shanker, former president of the American Federation of Teachers, a national teachers' union, articulated the basic structure of charter schools. He proposed that teachers could be freed from bureaucratic constraints and granted a "charter" to establish new kinds of public schools where teachers could experiment with new instructional methods. He proposed the idea to break the factory model of educational delivery which was dominated by traditional lectures and the expectation that all students would learn in the same way and at the same pace. His goal was that charter schools could serve as education laboratories, places where innovative instructional methods could be incubated and then implemented in other public schools. Administratively, Shanker kept charter schools under the control of the public school system, including the involvement of teachers' unions. Charter schools were to be approved by the local school board and operated by teachers within the public school system (Shanker 1988).

Readers may not recognize Shanker's vision in today's charter schools because most charter schools are run by individuals or organizations outside the public school system, including for-profit companies. Education reformers, in an effort to break the "exclusive franchise" of government-run public schools, radicalized Shanker's charter school idea by allowing these schools to be authorized by bodies separate and apart from local districts. Their intent was to expand the operation of charter schools to educational entrepreneurs outside the public school system and encourage competition between charter and traditional public schools (Kolderie 1990).

Charter schools—independently operated, publicly funded schools—are a hybrid between public and private schools. They are open to all students regardless of race, gender, ability, or disability. While students are required to apply to attend a charter school, the schools are prohibited from restricting admissions. If the number of student applicants exceeds the number of available spaces, charter schools are required to admit students according to a lottery that assigns each applicant an equal probability of selection. Also, unlike private schools, charter schools are prohibited from charging tuition. As independent schools, any organization can apply for a charter to establish and operate a charter school. Governing bodies are authorized

Charter schools—independently operated, publicly funded schools—are a hybrid between public and private schools.

to grant applicants the charter. Once granted, the charter is valid for up to fifteen years, depending on the state, and is renewable by the authorizing agency, assuming the school is in good standing. To maintain their charter and as a condition of renewal, charter schools must meet minimum requirements established by the state.

As independently run schools, charter schools are free from many of the laws and regulations that govern traditional public schools. Most common, they are often freed from the state budgeting and personnel regulations that school choice proponents argue create inefficiencies in the public school system. For example, charter schools may not be required to hire certified teachers or follow personnel rules such as collective bargaining agreements. They are, however, required to follow state academic requirements. They are responsible for teaching to state-approved academic standards, students are required to take standardized tests, and state school accountability policies apply to them. Private schools, by contrast, are autonomous schools that are not be required to follow all state laws because they are not authorized by the state.

School choice proponents and policymakers argue that charter schools are distinguished from traditional public schools based on the trade-off of increased flexibility for increased accountability. The schools are allowed to operate largely independent of state regulations in exchange for being held accountable to an authorizing body through the terms of their charter and competitive forces. Parental choice dictates if charter schools can attract and retain sufficient student enrollment counts to remain in operation. In this respect, charter schools are expected to respond to parent consumers like private businesses (Finn, Manno, and Vanourek 2000).

Politically, charter schools have gained in popularity in large part due to their bipartisan appeal. Policymakers on both sides of the political aisle have found common ground in charter schools to advance their cause. Republicans, with many school choice proponents among their ranks, seized charter schools as an opportunity to inject competition into public education and promote deregulation reforms. Democratic support for charter schools came from traditionally underserved communities that embraced charter schools as a means of improving low-quality public schools in their neighborhoods. For example, community organizations sought to leverage the flexibility afforded by charter school policies to build successful and culturally relevant schools in minority neighborhoods (Rofes and Stulberg 2004).

Between 1991 and 2001, thirty-nine states and the District of Columbia enacted charter school laws. By 2017, forty-five states and the District of Columbia had passed charter school laws, and there were more than sixty-seven hundred charter schools in the United States serving approximately 3 million students, or 5 percent of all public school students (National Center for Education Statistics 2017b). Charter schools represent a major advancement in school choice policy due to the speed in which policymakers embraced charter school laws, the rapid growth of these schools, and because in a few states, there are a sufficient number of charter schools to constitute a viable alternative sector of public schools. Arizona, for example, is home to over six hundred charter schools, representing 30 percent of all public schools and 17 percent of all public school students (Arizona Charter School Association 2017). When Hurricane Katrina destroyed hundreds of public schools in New Orleans, in 2005, policymakers replaced the public school system with an all-charter-school system (see https://educationresearchalliancenola.org for a history and ongoing research on New Orleans charter schools).

Charter schools can operate very differently from one state to the next because each state has crafted relevant laws to meet its specific needs and policy objectives. State laws detail the overarching purpose of charter schools, their funding structure, and how they interact with public school districts. In addition, individual state laws dictate which political bodies govern the schools, along with the processes by which schools are approved, held accountable, and renewed.

According to school choice advocates, states with strong charter school laws are those that empower multiple charter school authorizers that operate independent of local school districts and state authority, promote growth in the number of charter schools, allow school-level autonomy, and provide accessible and equitable funding for charter schools. In states with strong laws, charter schools are often framed as competitors to traditional public schools, and there are often more charter schools per capita than in states with weak charter school laws (National Alliance for Public Charter Schools 2017b).

Arizona has a strong charter school law, and these schools are positioned as competitors to traditional public schools. Policymakers leveraged charter school expansion to encourage an education marketplace by removing barriers to new charter school start-ups, empowering authorizing bodies to approve charter schools in any school district in the state without the permission of local school districts, exempting charter schools from most state requirements, including the requirement to hire certified teachers, and awarding organizations fifteen-year contracts to operate charter schools, the lengthiest such contracts in the country. Arizona parents are regarded as consumers and encouraged to vote with their feet by exiting traditional public schools in favor of charter schools. There are no caps on the number of charter schools in Arizona. The number and types of these schools are regulated by parental demand. Many pro–school choice organizations have hailed the state for its quick and massive expansion of charter schools, while others have characterized the state as the "wild west" of school choice where limited oversight has allowed the existence of too many questionable charter school operators and ineffective instructional practices (Maranto et al. 1999).

By contrast, several states have fewer than fifty operational charter schools. These states limit the number of charter schools by narrowing the number of charter school authorizing bodies, requiring approval of the local school district before opening a charter school, placing caps on the number of charter schools, and requiring charter schools to follow many of the same rules and regulations as traditional public schools, curtailing school-level autonomy.

Finally, the funding implications of charter schools are important to understand. In general, charter schools are funded by the state, which also provides significant funding for traditional public schools. In cases where charter schools are operated by organizations outside the public school system, public funds are directed away from traditional public schools. For example, in Arizona, where charter schools enroll 16 percent of the state student population, they receive 26 percent of state education funding (Arizona Department of Education 2016). Charter schools also have no taxing authority. Unlike traditional public schools, they cannot pass local bonds and overrides to fund school capital and operations.

Open Enrollment

Open enrollment is a form of school choice within the public school system and does not have an impact on or expand school choices outside the public school system to include private or charter schools. Open enrollment policies allow students to attend any public school within a district or within a state if space is available. The purpose of these policies is to dissolve geographic school attendance boundaries by freeing students from mandatory school assignments. In concept, open enrollment policies are intended to increase the number of quality public school options available to parents, which is viewed as a laudatory outcome for students living in communities with low-quality public schools. In practice, however, the ability of families to participate in open enrollment is limited by availability (the higher-quality schools are the most likely to be filled to capacity) and the logistical constraints families face to transport their students to schools farther away from their home.

Open enrollment policies have received less attention and are less controversial than other school choice policies because student participation does not necessarily result in reduced funding for the local school district. Under open enrollment, all public funds remain within the public school system. In some states, open enrollment is limited to public schools within a student's school district of residence. In these cases, the amount per pupil allotted to the school district remains unaffected when students participate in open enrollment. The distribution of resources at the school level, however, can be altered to provide additional funds to districts and schools with higher student enrollment counts. In other states, open enrollment is broader, and students can enroll in any public school in the state, meaning that students can attend public schools outside their school district of residence. In these cases, the exit of students from one school district to another results in less state funding for the school district of exit as the allotted per pupil amount is provided to the school district of entry.

As of 2016, forty-six states had open enrollment polices. The number of students attending a public school through open enrollment is unknown because most states do not require school districts to track open enrollment counts (Education Commission of the States 2016a). In addition, in a market environment where school districts are encouraged to compete for students to increase funding, open enrollment is regarded as another strategy for school districts to increase student counts by attracting students from other districts. School districts commonly advertise the quality of their public schools to students outside the district and may (but are often not required to) offer transportation to ease the logistical constraints of attending schools that may be located far from their home.

Education Savings Accounts

Education savings accounts (ESAs) are the most recent school choice policy; as of 2017, only five states had these programs. ESAs allow eligible families to opt out of enrolling their children in a public school. Instead, families can access 90 percent of the allotted state per pupil amount that would have been spent on their children if they had enrolled in a public school. The state deposits the funds directly into a privately managed bank account, where parents can expend the funds on any qualifying education-related service they choose. Parents are not required to expend all funds in the academic year in which they are distributed. The funds can be rolled over across years, and if state law permits, the funds can be used for future educational expenses, including postsecondary costs such as college tuition.

ESAs operate similar to vouchers in that they designate a specified amount of money per pupil for parents to access for school choice purposes. Unlike vouchers, however, the ESA funds are distributed directly to parents, who choose where to spend the money. They, not the state, pay the ESA funds directly to educational providers. Thus, when parents expend funds at private or religious schools, the government is not distributing those funds to religious schools. This two-step process, where the state provides funds to parents and parents spend it directly with education providers, is the primary reason that ESAs have been found constitutional, even in states with a Blaine amendment that expressly prohibits state governments from funding religious schools with public money.

The policy implications of ESAs are considerable. First, the state's role is more limited under ESAs than any other school choice policy. This role shifts from funding and providing public education to providing the funding that parents use to purchase a range of alternative educational services for their child. The state is tasked with developing the list of allowable educational services that parents can purchase using ESA funds—broad categories such as tuition and fees, educational therapies, transportation, and supplies. The state is not required, however, to approve educational providers or establish minimal requirements for these providers to receive ESA funds.

Parents have considerable latitude to purchase educational services for their children as they see appropriate. Advocates argue that ESAs provide an opportunity for parents to tailor or individualize the education of their student by purchasing a menu of services (Ladner 2012). For example, parents can spend funds on private school tuition and educational therapies or any other combination of services that they choose. Others question this shift, asking if under ESAs, the state is subverting "its constitutional obligation to provide adequately for public education, thereby converting a child's right to an education to merely the right to shop for one" (Mead 2015, 705).

Second, ESA programs have minimal reporting requirements for participants and feature little, if any, academic or financial state oversight. Parents are required to submit an expenditure report to the state that details the amounts spent on each educational service provider. Students are not required, however, to complete academic assessments, such as standardized tests, to track their learning and progress. In addition, there are no requirements that educational providers demonstrate performance or academic success. The lack of accountability means that there is no method to evaluate the effectiveness of ESA programs. Critics argue that absent academic and financial accountability requirements like those in public schools, there is effectively no oversight of public funds.

Proponents argue that ESAs are indeed accountable—to parents: "Parent accountability affects the supply side of the education choice equation. Families choose to enroll their children in a particular private school or utilize an array of education-related services, and if they're unhappy with the quality of services received, they simply can take their children and ESA funds to another education provider" (Burke 2013, 8). This argument is consistent with Friedman's shift of responsibility from the state to individual families.

Third, the cost implications of ESAs are complex. Proponents argue that ESAs are structured to provide a cost savings to the state because only 90 percent of what students would have received had they attended a public school is deposited in the ESA account, leaving 10 percent to use on other state priorities. In addition, ESAs are funded through state allocations, meaning that local school districts save the local portion of school funding. The potential cost savings of the ESA program to the state is a benefit that school choice proponents cite to make the argument that even students who do not participate in the ESA program benefit from the involvement of those who do participate (Ladner 2012). No research or legislative reports, however, document the actual cost savings to the state except for budgetary estimates.

Critics argue that there are cost implications to ESAs. To begin, ESAs divert public funds from public education at the district and school levels. While there may be overall cost savings at the state level, the local public schools where students would have attended receive less funding when students participate in the ESA program. Also, with fewer students enrolled, local public schools may not be able to take advantage of economies of scale that help lower the per pupil costs of providing educational services. For example, if a public school enrolls two special education students, the funds from both students contribute to the cost of hiring the teacher. If one student participates in an ESA program, the school is still required to hire a teacher to provide education services to the remaining student, but funds from only one student, rather than two, are available to cover the cost. Also, policymakers in states where ESAs are expanded at the same time that public school budgets are cut should prioritize their obligation to adequately fund public schools, including charter schools, before establishing alternative programs that divert funds out of the public school system (Garcia 2012).

Finally, ESAs are likely to result in larger educational inequities than vouchers because under an ESA program, students potentially receive less than they would under a voucher program. Like vouchers, ESAs may be an unrealistic choice for many low-income students because they are unable to afford the full costs associated with attending a private school.

There is very little research on ESAs because they are a new development and the lack of academic accountability requirements makes it difficult to conduct research on the ESA programs in existence. The available evidence is from parent self-report surveys and expenditure reports in Arizona, the state with the longest-running and most expansive ESA program. These sources indicate that the preponderance of ESA funds is spent on private school tuition. Approximately a third of parents purchase more than one educational service, such as tuition at a private school and tutoring. Commonly, some ESA funds are unspent and remain available for parents to use in a later year (Burke 2013). Finally, there are indications that students who participate in the Arizona ESA program were enrolled in school districts with higher percentages of white students and wealthier than the general student population.

School Choice by the Numbers

Despite the popularity and growth of school choice programs, traditional public schools greatly outnumber schools of choice. In 2014, there were 98,271 traditional public schools compared to 33,619 private schools, by far the most common schools of choice. Since 2001, however, the number of private schools has declined slightly. Charter schools are the fastest-growing school choice option. From 2001 to 2014, the number of charter schools increased by 250 percent (see figure 1). The number of traditional public schools, by comparison, increased by 5.4 percent during this same time period.

The number of students enrolled in charter schools has also grown rapidly, increasing 460 percent since 2001 (see figure 2). By comparison, enrollment in magnet schools has ebbed and flowed, ultimately increasing over the same time period, and private school enrollment has declined. Student enrollment in traditional public schools, which

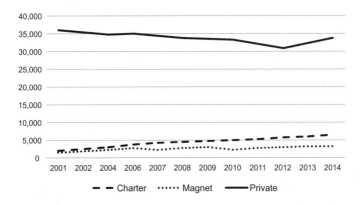

Figure 1 Number of charter, magnet, and private schools by select academic years, 2001–2014.

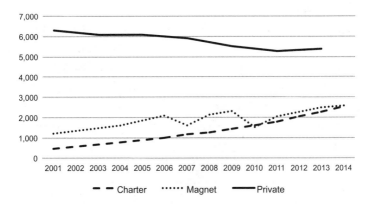

Figure 2 Student enrollment (in thousands) by charter, magnet, and private schools, select academic years, 2001–2014.

totaled almost 49 million students in 2015, has grown by 5.6 percent since 2001.

A Reference Guide to School Choice Policies

Table 1 is a reference guide to understanding and differentiating school choice policies (see also *The ABCs of School Choice*, https://www.edchoice.org/research/the-abcs-of-school-choice/). The first set of columns details the role of government under each policy: funding, providing, and regulating the delivery of public education. The second set of columns indicates whether under each policy, student attendance remains within the public school system or if students are allowed to attend schools outside the public school system. The third column indicates if students have access to either private providers or private schools. The last column details the status of public funds under each policy. Does funding stay within the public school system as students exercise choice or leave the public school system?

Using public schools as the baseline structure of public education, one can understand how school choice policies transform the structure and delivery of public education. In the case of traditional public schools, the role of government is to fund, provide, and regulate public education. Student attendance is limited to public

Table 1 Summary of school choice policies, major provisions

	Role of Government in Education			Student Attendance		Access to Private Schools/Providers	Funding
	Fund	Provide	Regulate	Within	Outside		
Traditional public	X	X	X	X			Stay
Home school					X	X	—
Private					X	X	—
Magnet	X	X	X	X			Stay
Open enrollment	X	X	X	X			Stay
Charter	X		X		X		Exit
Voucher	X		X		X	X	Exit
ESA	X				X	X	Exit

schools, and all funding remains within the public school system.

In home schooling and private school arrangements, the oldest schooling alternatives, parents assume responsibility for their student's education; there is no governmental role. There are also limited funding implications because home-schooled and private school students were never enrolled in a public school to generate public funds.

Under public school choice options (magnet schools and open enrollment), the baseline structure of the public school system remains unchanged. Students are not required to attend their neighborhood public school, but all student attendance and funding remains within the public school system. In addition, government maintains maximum control of delivering public education.

By comparison, charter schools are funded and regulated by government through contractual arrangements with public governing bodies. Students move outside the public school system to enroll in independently operated charter schools, although these schools are not private. When students attend a charter school, funding follows the student and exits the public school system.

Under voucher programs, the role of government is to fund individual parental choices and provide limited regulation to ensure that participating private schools meet minimal requirements. Students enroll in private schools outside the public school system. and funding exits the public school system.

Under ESAs, the government's role is limited to funding public education; it has no authority in delivering that education. Students move outside the public school system, and public funding exits with the student to private schools and providers.

Conclusion

As a result of school choice policies, parents have more schooling options available now than at any other time in American history. In states with extensive school choice policies, parents can choose to home-school their children or send them to the local neighborhood public school, a public school in another school district, a charter school, or a private school paid for (at least in part) by public funds. School choice options are very popular with parents, and policymakers are likely to continue expanding these policies in the future.

This chapter provided an overview of the major school choice policies in US public education with an emphasis on how these policies are tied to school desegregation and influence the role and responsibilities of individuals versus government as it pertains to the delivery of public education.

The following chapter places school choice policies in the broader context of education reform to discuss how proponents present choice as a way to improve public education for all students. The chapter also addresses the many questions and concerns about the extent to which school choice can deliver on its promises and the possibility that it may exacerbate educational inequalities.

THE PILLARS OF SCHOOL CHOICE ARGUMENTS

This chapter discusses the major arguments that support school choice policies. For each argument, I present the underlying problem in education that the choice is intended to address and then review the arguments that school choice proponents have put forth to address the problem. I also present the counterarguments but do not judge the merits of them. Rather, my goal is to equip readers with an understanding of the major arguments on both sides so they can assess the merits themselves.

In general, school choice policies are considered a way to promote reform in public education. Attempts to reform American public education have existed nearly as long as public education itself. There are too many policies, practices, and ideas that have fallen under the umbrella of education reform to provide a thorough treatment in this book. For our purpose, it is sufficient to define education reform as attempts, through laws, regulations, or policies, to dismantle the status quo policies and practices associated with the administration and delivery of public education at a specific time. Education reformers have addressed different issues depending on the state of education at the time. For example, the earliest accounts of education reform date back to the 1800s when Horace Mann led the common school movement, shifting control of education from rural schoolhouses to the state to develop a uniform system of education and giving rise to the structure of today's public school system (Brouillette 1999).

I also do not discuss the extent to which the issues that education reforms purport to address actually exist or assess the extent to which these issues are the most important or appropriate to improve public education according to the research. The existence and importance of the issues that reformers believe plague public education are based as much on tradition and reputation as they are on tangible research evidence. To complicate matters, the debates about the underlying causes of the issues facing public education and the most appropriate means to address them play out in the public and political arenas where sound bites are often more persuasive than academic research. The important point here is this: people in positions of authority believe that the issues with public education discussed in this chapter are of sufficient importance to be addressed through changes in education policy, and they have convinced public and the political actors to address these issues with school choice.

The arguments that school choice can effectively address these issues are often based on long-held beliefs, personal experiences, and philosophical grounds that are not easily refutable with research evidence, and I will not do so here. Rather, I present the arguments and counterarguments associated with school choice common to the public discourse, so readers are equipped to understand and evaluate them on their own accord.

Finally, education reform and school choice policies are politically charged issues that evoke heated responses from both camps. I do my best to distill the arguments and counterarguments to their core tenets, absent finger pointing or personal attacks. Some will take exception to this approach or my attempt to depoliticize the discussion because they argue that the core principles at play in the promotion of school choice are inherently political: greed, prejudice, and power. My intent is to cut through the political rhetoric to present the core issues at play in school choice debates.

The four primary arguments put forth in support of school choice are the elimination of government bureaucracies, the interjection of competition into education through market forces, the promotion of parental choice as the most granular form of local control, and school choice as the "new" civil rights issue of our time.

Eliminating Government Bureaucracies

The advancement of school choice policies is part of a larger discussion about reducing government bureaucracies. Economists have long argued that the delivery of public services could be improved if providers were freed from the stifling constraints of bureaucratic organizations. Bureaucracies are characterized by hierarchical authority structures, a rigid division of labor among employees, and adherence to the administration of rules, regulations, and procedures. They are operated through standardized processes that contribute to their reputation as impersonal, inflexible organizations that react slowly to the external environment. They are also considered inefficient because employees, often referred to as bureaucrats, tend to generate busywork or red tape as a means of justifying their existence such that additional effort by employees does not yield commensurate output. The benefit of bureaucracies is that they provide an ordered means to organize many people and several individual units under a single organizational structure. Bureaucracies are also more predictable, more meritocratic, and less subjective than more informal structures, such as those based on personal relationships.

The organizational structure of the current educational system originated in the Industrial Revolution (1740–1840) that transformed how Americans worked and lived. During this period, work processes were organized around a factory system with a defined division of labor and more specialized functions. These trends influenced the development of many governmental structures, including public education.

During this period, public education transformed from disparate rural schools to bureaucratic governance structures. In the years following the Industrial Revolution, school administrators were confronted with organizing the delivery of public education to the burgeoning student populations that had migrated to urban areas. They addressed this challenge by creating networks of schools governed by a central governmental bureaucracy, the school district. The best practices at the time, promoted by the education reformers of the day, sought to implementation the "one best system" of education designed by professionals and delivered in modernized schools. Reformers pressed for standardized teaching and learning practices, the centralization of decision-making authority to education experts and professionalized school boards, and hierarchical organizational structures modeled after corporations (Tyack and Cuban 1995):

> From 1910 to 1960 the number of one-room schools declined from approximately 200,000 to 20,000. In trying to modernize rural schooling they believed that children as well as teachers would benefit, and

indeed the students did gain better school buildings,
a broader and more contemporary course studies,
and better qualified teachers and administrators.
(Tyack 1974, 25)

The by-product of bureaucratic school governance,
however, was the establishment of large, centralized bureaucracies, particularly in urban areas. The operational
shortcomings and injustices of school district bureaucracies are well documented in academic articles and mainstream media publications, which are beyond the scope
of this book (Callahan 1962; Howard 2012). The major
conclusion of this literature for our discussion of school
choice is that a strong case has been made, particularly
in the court of public opinion, that while school district
bureaucracies were once considered novel reforms in education, they are now regarded as entrenched features of
an antiquated public school system. When reformers refer
to dismantling the status quo in education, they are most
often referring to eliminating the role and influence of
school district bureaucracies (Bolick 2017).

Bureaucracies also extend to the school level, where
rules and regulations govern nearly all aspects of school
operations. In the classroom, the uniform practices of
bureaucratic organizations are manifest in standardized teaching and learning practices. The result is a factory model of educational delivery where consistent

When reformers refer to dismantling the status quo in education, they are most often referring to eliminating the role and influence of school district bureaucracies.

teaching practices, namely, the delivery of education through teacher-led lectures, are applied to all students, regardless of ability, interest, or proclivity, in an effort to achieve a standardized educational output, such as passing a standardized test or meeting seat time requirements. This standardized approach to education, which was once promoted for its uniformity and efficiency, is now widely criticized as impersonal, rigid, and stifling to innovative teaching and learning practices (Kimbrough and Todd 1967).

Since *Brown*, and faced with becoming the vanguard of racial integration, school districts' bureaucracies have applied the policies and practices with which they were most familiar at the time to address this highly contentious issue. Characteristic of bureaucratic organizations, they developed standardized procedures that were then applied to all students, such as mandated attendance boundaries and busing. These policies were deaf to individual parental preferences and contributed to the perception of schools as impersonal organizations. When parents demanded that their personal preferences be accounted for in school attendance decisions, this level of individualization was difficult to accomplish in the ordered, slow-changing environment of large bureaucratic structures. Most recently, schools have been criticized for reacting slowly to technological advances in content delivery and failing to move away from traditional practices, such as teacher-led lecture formats and seat time requirements.

Thus, when critics began a movement toward eliminating bureaucratic structures, public education was a logical target for change. Collectively, the public school system is the largest governmental bureaucracy in the United States, and public education is the largest expenditure in many state budgets. The movement to reduce school district bureaucracies through school choice is based on the premise that schools would be better-run organizations if they were freed from stifling government rules and regulations. Once freed from bureaucratic constraints, they would operate more efficiently, become more responsive to the external environment, particularly parents, and would promote rather than stifle innovation (Finn, Manno, and Vanourek 2000).

The argument that school choice policies could free schools from bureaucratic constraints has played out most forcefully in the case for charter schools. School choice proponents and policymakers argued that charter schools should be freed from bureaucratic control based on the trade-off of increased flexibility for increased accountability. For this reason, strong charter school laws—those viewed by school choice proponents as advantageous to the expansion of charter schools—are characterized by providing charter schools as much flexibility as possible through exemptions from as many state laws and regulations as possible. In exchange for more flexibility and less direct governmental oversight, these schools are expected to be held more accountable than traditional public schools. They are accountable to both an authorizing body through the terms of their charter contract and to parents, who are expected to vote with their feet to enroll in the best school for their child, dictating which schools could attract and retain sufficient student enrollment counts to remain in operation. In this way, school choice proponents argue that charter schools will be responsive to the external environment, parent consumers, in a manner more similar to private businesses than governmental bureaucracies (Nathan 1996; Finn et al. 2000).

While the discussion of bureaucracies and regulations may appear to be the fodder of policy wonks alone, the debate over the potential of charter schools to reform the bureaucratic public education system has attracted mainstream media attention in the United States, bringing school choice to the public consciousness. The popular and award-winning 2013 documentary, *Waiting for Superman*, takes aim at school bureaucracies and the factory model of education for rigidness and propensity toward standardization over innovation. In the film, teachers' unions are presented as the antagonists for supporting stagnant bureaucracies over the best interests of students. The protagonists are individual students who are portrayed as trapped in low-performing and dysfunctional schools and await the outcome of a lottery to attend a charter school. Charter schools are portrayed as innovative, high-quality educational environments.

In practice, many aspects of charter schools have developed as proponents envisioned. They are a viable alternative to public schools and a viable education sector in many states in large part due to bipartisan support. As intended, these schools operate in a less-regulated environment than traditional public schools do. And many parents are making the choice to send their children to these schools. (Charter school outcomes and discussed in more detail in chapter 3.)

Nevertheless, the implementation of charter school has been curtailed relative to the original intentions of proponents. They have not been given flexibility across all operations, which bears on their ability to implement innovative programs. In general, charter schools have received the most flexibility with respect to administrative, financial, and personnel policies. They are still required to follow state regulations governing academics and state-mandated assessments (Finnigan 2007). They are also required to align their curricula and teach the same academic standards as traditional public schools do, and their students are required to take and pass the same state-mandated standardized tests as traditional public school students. Charter schools are also held to the same school accountability requirements as traditional public schools.

The consistency among traditional public and charter schools with respect to academics and assessments means that parents do not have the ability to select a charter school that meets their full private interests. They can choose among charter schools that are all required to teach and be held accountable to the same academic standards as traditional public schools. For example, there are no options where parents can enroll their child in a charter school to learn a foreign language in lieu of English. There may be a charter school with a bilingual or dual-language emphasis where a foreign language is prevalent, but the charter school is still expected to teach to the same language arts standards and students are required to take the same language arts standardized assessment as every other charter or traditional public school in the state.

By design, charter school–authorizing bodies took a hands-off approach to monitoring and enforcement, relying heavily on parental choice to regulate the availability of charter schools in local communities. In the first decade of rapid charter school growth, a flurry of research on the sponsoring and monitoring activities of charter school authorizers revealed that in practice, the hands-off approach to oversight was failing to hold charter schools accountable (Fusarelli 2001). Many charter school authorizers were understaffed (SRI International 2002) or staffed by personnel with insufficient experience to fulfill their new roles. The vague language of many charter school statutes also left authorizers and schools unclear with respect to the division of their responsibilities in a newly deregulated environment (Hill et al. 2001). The technical requirements for creating clear academic performance goals and the demands of measuring academic goals with credible assessments were beyond the expertise of many charter school directors and authorizers (Griffin and Wohlstetter 2001).

The ultimate form of accountability, closing poorly performing charter schools, proved much more difficult than school choice proponents theorized. Certainly some charter schools were closed due to academic performance, but school closures were too few to bolster a persuasive argument that charter authorizers were holding up their end of the great trade-off between flexibility and accountability. Critics also charged that the trade-off of charter schools narrowed the public's role in these schools. For example, charter school board members are often appointed, not elected, and taxpayer-citizens have limited means to assert their voice in school operations. In market arrangements, disgruntled parents are given preferential treatment because, as consumers, they can threaten to move, depriving the school of resources. The average taxpayer-citizen, however, is not a parent and faces a more circuitous route to influence charter school operations. Charter schools do not have the same incentives to respond to the average taxpayer-citizen as they do the parent-consumer because the taxpayer-citizen does not have a direct financial impact on the school. In addition, the average taxpayer-citizen cannot use the ballot box to influence school leadership by voting to replace charter school board members (Lubienski 2001).

Market Competition

School choice is seen as a means of interjecting market-based competition into the public school system in order to exert external pressures to reform public education. Here, education reformers are employing school choice policies to break up government-operated public school monopolies. In many communities, government-run school districts are the only organization that establishes and administers public schools. Government public school monopolies developed for two major reasons. First, states are responsible for public education and governmental entities were established to carry out this obligation. Second, there is a high cost associated with building and operating schools, leaving the state as the logical option to fund the infrastructure to provide public education.

Monopolies are considered inefficient and an inferior option for consumers because they are criticized for producing lower-quality goods at a higher price than in a competitive market environment. With respect to education, the argument against a state-administered monopoly is that schools and school districts have little incentive to cut costs and improve operations with respect to administrative procedures and classroom practices.

To break up monopolies, education reformers have advocated for school choice policies that inject market-based competition into public schools from outside the public school system. Similar to private markets where competition is associated with lower costs and increased product quality, school choice policies are expected to encourage schools to improve the delivery of education once they are forced to compete for students and the per-pupil funding that comes with student enrollment.

To foster competition, school choice proponents seek to develop an education marketplace composed of multiple education providers. For this reason, they widen the pool of prospective providers to include nongovernmental entities such as nonprofit organizations, for-profit organizations, and private schools. They contend that in a market environment, all schools, public and private alike, will operate more efficiently, at lower cost, and will be more responsive to the needs of families than the traditional, monopolistic public school system will.

Competition in an education market is intended to improve the quality of schools directly and indirectly. The direct influence is through an increase in the number of high-quality schools available to students. Students

To foster competition, school choice proponents seek to develop an education marketplace composed of multiple education providers.

who enroll in a high-quality school of choice have a direct benefit: they are expected to receive a better education than if they attended a traditional public school. There is also an indirect benefit through competition: market-driven policies are expected to improve the quality of educational delivery of all schools to the benefit of all students, even students who do not participate in school choice and remain enrolled in a traditional public school. The prevailing idea is that under a market environment, competition from outside education providers will exert competitive pressures on public schools to improve the quality of education in an effort to attract and retain students. In this way, even students who do not take advantage of school choice by exiting the public school system will benefit because the public schools in general have improved in order to remain competitive. In an education market, school choice is intended to be the rising tide that lifts all boats, meaning that both choosers and non-choosers alike are expected to benefit from competition (Hoxby 2001).

The economic principles at work in a competitive market system are fundamentally based on the ideas of Adam Smith and the invisible hand that Smith argued guides economic activity in a free market economy. According to Smith, in a free exchange of goods and services, offered most efficiently in a market environment, individual self-interest is the most influential driver of economic activity

and societies as a whole benefit from the rational behavior of individual consumers pursuing their economic
self-interest (Smith 2000). The faith in markets and the
behavior of individual consumers to foster a collective
benefit is a deeply held American belief.

To illustrate how markets and competition are intended to work in education, a noneducation example is
helpful. In this hypothetical example, let's assume there
are two coffee shops in a small town: coffee shop A serves a
higher-quality cup of coffee than coffee shop B. We'll make
two more assumptions to apply this example to education:
(1) consumers agree on what constitutes a better cup of
coffee and (2) the price for a cup of coffee is fixed. The
rational consumer, in an effort to purchase the best possible cup of coffee, is expected to patronize coffee shop A
in favor of coffee shop B. Collectively, the rational actions
of individual consumers should result in more customers
for coffee shop A, along with increased revenue. Commen-
surately, coffee shop B should experience a decline in customers and revenue. At this point, coffee shop B has two
general options: it can close due to low consumer demand
or improve its product—serve a better cup of coffee—to
attract new consumers or draw consumers away from coffee shop A. There is a collective benefit to all coffee drink-
ers because in either case, the quality of coffee in our
hypothetical small town is improved due to the individual
actions of rational consumers. If coffee shop B closes,

the only remaining coffee shop is the one that serves the higher-quality cup of coffee. If coffee shop B improves to compete with coffee shop A, the town has two high-quality coffee shops.

School choice advocates who seek to interject market competition to improve education make a similar argument. The education example goes as follows: In an education marketplace where there are several school options, individual parents are encouraged to vote with their feet and choose the highest-quality school for their child. Thus, higher-quality schools will experience an increase in student demand as more students seek admission, and lower-quality schools will experience a decline in student enrollment due to lower demand. The lower-quality school is expected to either close due to low student enrollment or improve in quality. In either case, the quality of public schools in general is improved because either only high-quality public schools remain in existence or lower-quality public schools have improved in response.

The applicability of a private market analogy to public education brings up a number of critical policy questions. To begin, education is a complex good. Unlike coffee, there is no easily agreeable definition of a quality public school. What one parent values in the education of his or her child may be very different from what another parent values. If parents select schools for different reasons or schools do not understand clearly why students left, then the market signals are distorted and schools are not clear about how they must improve to "compete" for students. Also, what if individual parental preferences are counter to public purposes? For example, how are public schools to react if parents choose private schools because they prefer their student to be taught specific religious values? Public schools cannot provide a religious education to meet parent demand. Or what if parents choose schools based largely on the racial/ethnic composition of the student body? Public schools cannot deny students on the basis of race/ethnicity, among other characteristics.

It is important to note that the general assumption among pro–school choice policymakers and advocates is that parents will engage in consumer-like behavior in an education market. Specifically, parents are expected to make school choice decisions based on maximizing the academic outcomes for their student. For this reason, states publish school report cards to help inform parental school choice decisions. The report cards include academic achievement data, such as standardized test scores and graduation rates, along with information on school programs. The practical question is to what extent parents base their school choice decisions on state-sponsored school report cards over more informal sources such as word-of-mouth or Internet groups.

Also, there are questions about the practicability of competition to force school closures in public education.

School closures are not analogous to a business closure. In the case of a business closure, states are not required to provide an alternative business for its citizens. States, however, are required to provide public education so students can't be left without a public school. Unlike a private market environment, states are ultimately required to provide all students with a public school. Thus, even in when a local public school is underperforming, states cannot rely on outside organizations or the market alone to educate students.

Proponents also point out that choice in a market functions in two ways that could lead to the stratification of students by academic ability. While school choice advocates place an emphasis on the ability of parents to choose schools, opponents point out that in a market environment, schools also choose students. Through mechanisms such as marketing, strategic placement of campuses, and student recruitment, schools play an active role in shaping the composition of their student bodies by influencing which students seek admission and which do not (Lubienski 2007; Bancroft 2009). For example, BASIS is a large and well-known network of US charter schools, commonly recognized as among the best public schools in the United States (US News and World Report 2017). The BASIS network advertises its schools as providing an academically rigorous education (http://basisschools.org). Critics charge that targeted advertisements like the BASIS approach may dissuade low-performing students from applying for admission.

Because students with disabilities and English-language learners require more resources to educate and generally perform lower on standardized tests than regular education students, some charge that high-performing charter schools may be discouraged from enrolling these students in an effort to maintain superior test scores (McEwan 2000). Proponents of this view also argue that charter schools push out low-performing students by encouraging them to leave in order to maintain higher-performing students, while traditional public schools are left to educate more low-performing students even though empirical evidence indicates that these students are not more likely to leave a charter than a traditional school (Zimmer and Guarino 2013).

Finally, opponents argue that markets are inequitable and should not be the driving force of public education (Henig 1994). In a market environment, there are high- and low-quality options available of many goods and services. This inequity is not regarded as a problem to ameliorate; rather, it's a predictable outcome of consumers spending based on their level of income. Proponents of school choice argue that education markets would inevitably lead to lower-quality schooling options in poorer neighborhoods than in higher-income neighborhoods.

Parental Choice

Local control, which has a long-standing and strong tradition in the United States, holds that the best policy decisions are made at the most local level possible. Policies that purport to adhere to the ideals of local control seek to empower those most affected by policies to control the decisions on those policies. Local control proponents do not hold top-down policies in high regard because they are considered out of touch with the preferences of the individuals most affected by those policies.

Unlike many other countries, US public education is not controlled at the national level; rather, it is the responsibility of individual states. Although the structure of public education can differ considerably from one state to the next, all states share one common form of local control: locally elected school boards that hold significant policy- and decision-making authority over the schools in their jurisdiction. School boards are incorporated at the county, city, and even community levels. These boards came into existence to provide community input and expertise to school operations, and although some argue that their influence is diminishing under the expanded authority of state and federal policies, school boards and the local control remain prominent and influential in US public education (Shober and Hartney 2014).

Parental choice can be considered the most granular form of local control in public education. The argument in favor of expanding choice is based on the idea that no one knows the interests and abilities of students better than their parents, and so parents, they argue, are in the best position to advocate for their children. Thus, school choice advocates contend that parents should be empowered to make as many decisions as possible on behalf of their child, most important of which is choosing the school that best meets the needs of their child.

The sentiment is best expressed by school choice advocates themselves. According to EdChoice, a pro–school choice advocacy organization:

> For too long, parents have been told to sit down, be quiet and let the professionals handle their kids. Policymakers have similarly been bullied by those who seek to protect and preserve an educational system that has chronically failed many of those who most depend on it as their pathway to a successful life. (https://www.edchoice.org/who-we-are/our-mission/)

The strong reaction against top-down control among school choice advocates arises from a dissatisfaction with school district mandates that are perceived as muting parental preferences. Historically, school districts responded

The argument in favor of expanding parental choice is based on the idea that no one knows the interests and abilities of students better than their parents.

to desegregation orders with universal mandates that were unpopular among many parents, and education reformers have long railed against standardized teaching and learning conditions in public school classrooms. Thus, school choice policies that encouraged parental choice, such as Friedman's shift of educational responsibility from the state to individual families, were met with a receptive audience by frustrated policymakers and parents alike. When school district officials protested the shift in decision-making authority to the parental level, they were labeled traditionalists who were defending the status quo in opposition to change and innovation.

Many issues arise from relying heavily on parental preferences to drive education policy. The first is how to hold public schools accountable in an environment driven by parental choice. For many school choice advocates, parental choice is the ultimate form of accountability. The argument is that if a parent chooses a specific school or a specific educational service for his or her student, there is little place for the state to question that decision, even if the state has a compelling argument that the parental choice is not in the best interest of the student. The local control tradition holds that parents know what is best for their child, and state bureaucrats, who are removed from the situation, are not in a position to override these decisions. For this reason, parents have considerable latitude under school choice policies to make school choice decisions. School choice policies are agnostic on whether parents choose good or bad schools or whether parents choose high-quality educational services for their children.

The assumption behind market-based policies is that parents would exit low-performing schools in sufficient numbers to force low-quality schools to close. Yet the market process is neither immediate nor perfect, and schools of choice designated by the state as low performing remain in operation because parents continue to choose to send their children to such schools (Bell 2009). Even when charter schools violated the terms of their contracts and faced closure by their authorizing body, parents continued to send their children to those schools and fought to keep them open (Hess 2001). From a market perspective, the question becomes what role, if any, the state has to override parental choice and close low-performing schools if parents are choosing to send their students to such schools.

Confidence in parental choice is also a major reason there are essentially no checks on parental decisions under education savings accounts (ESAs) programs where the government has no oversight role and there are no external accountability requirements. Under ESA programs, parents are not required to demonstrate that their student is making academic progress, and educational service providers that receive ESA funds are not required to demonstrate their effectiveness or meet minimal requirements.

The expanded role of parental choice has been defended in court as a "circuit breaker" where "an exercise of parental choice renders permissible what would be legally impermissible if adopted by a governmental authority" (Mead and Lewis 2016, 101). In other words, parents can make educational choices even in instances where if state were to make the same choice, it would be illegal. The legality of parental choice as a circuit breaker is the reason that the two-step process under ESA programs (public funds provided directly to parents by the state and parents purchasing educational services directly) is a critical progression from school vouchers. Under an ESA program, states do not directly fund nonpublic institutions, including religious schools. Rather, because parents are choosing to expend ESA funds by paying for tuition in private religious schools, their choice is the circuit breaker that makes the ultimate transfer of funds to religious schools legal. The two-step process of ESA programs has been defended as constitutional even in states with Blaine amendments that prohibit direct government aid to religious educational institutions (Niehaus v. Huppenthal 2012). For this reason, I anticipate that ESA programs, rather than vouchers, will be expanded in the future. The legal precedent is set to allow policymakers seeking to provide students access to private religious schools through school choice policies to accomplish their goals through ESA programs.

School Choice as the "New" Civil Rights

The final argument in favor of school choice involves a broader interpretation of *Brown v. Board of Education*. This interpretation holds that segregation should not be regarded as the terminal outcome of the court's decision. Rather, the purpose of desegregating schools was to provide black students with educational opportunities on par with those of white students. Thus, advocates argue that school choice can increase the number of high-quality school options for minority students and that the freedom to access schools of choice is a contemporary civil rights issue. School choice proponents maintain that

> the meaning of civil rights is to live life free from discrimination on the grounds of race, sex, religion, age or disability. What can be more expressive of civil rights than to have the freedom, without government interference, to send our children to a school of our choice? (http://opportunitylives.com/charter-schools-and-choice-the-civil-rights-issue-of-our-day/)

The argument that school choice is a civil rights issue is most often discussed as the right of low-income or minority students to have the choice to exit traditionally poorly performing schools, particularly traditional public

Thus, advocates argue that school choice can increase the number of high-quality school options for minority students and that the freedom to access schools of choice is a contemporary civil rights issue.

schools, to enroll in the school of their choice. For example, President Trump's call for expanded school choice is consistent with the argument that school choice is a civil rights issue that benefits minority and low-income students. In his first speech to a joint session of Congress, he called education "the civil rights of our time" and encouraged Congress to pass an education bill that funds school choice for disadvantaged and minority students. He argued that "these families should be free to choose the public, private, charter, magnet, religious, or home school that is right for them" (Trump 2017). President Trump then singled out a young African American girl named Denisha and explained her struggles in school, including failing third grade twice. He pointed out that Denisha is now the first in her family to finish high school and college due to her enrollment in what he referred to as a "great" private learning center that she was able to attend with the help of a tax credit and a scholarship program. President Trump's school choice proposal and Denisha's story were greeted with enthusiastic applause.

The connection between school choice and civil rights has been advanced by more than school choice advocates. The sprawling roots of the charter school movement also are fixed to community schools, another public school choice initiative advanced by minority organizations. In the 1970s, black activists founded community schools out of frustration with failed desegregation policies.

They demanded community control over their public schools, a mission shared by many contemporary charter schools that serve black students (Rofes and Stulberg 2004). The community school perspective offers self-determination as a mechanism for educational reform where black communities can leverage the autonomy afforded by charter school policies to build successful and culturally relevant educational opportunities (Murrell 1999).

The perspective of charter schools as community schools reopens the debate on the goal of *Brown* to reveal the tensions between desegregation and educational equality. If one interprets the goal of *Brown* as strictly desegregation, then there is obvious concern for how charter schools exacerbate segregation by sanctioning the existence of predominantly black charter schools. If one interprets *Brown* as advancing educational equality, then charter schools represent an opportunity for communities to establish educational alternatives in cases where district schools have failed to improve the quality of education for black students (Stulberg 2006). Black charter school parents may not react negatively to single-race charter schools if students are receiving a quality education (Yancey 2004). For example, according to the director of a predominantly black charter school in North Carolina, "I hear parents say: 'My kid is reading a year above grade level. I don't care whether he is sitting next to a White student or not'" (Schnaiberg 1998, 22).

Advocates argue that school choice has the potential to break the strong relationship between a student's zip code and academic achievement outcomes. The relationship in question is based on the correlation between student achievement outcomes and student socioeconomic status (SES), where the latter is a measure of a family's economic and social position based on income, education, and parent occupation. High-SES families are those with higher incomes and parents who have completed more advanced education levels and have better connected social circles compared to low-SES families. While the research on the relationship between student academic achievement and SES is extensive and covers decades of studies, the basic finding is that students from higher-SES families perform better on academic achievement indicators such as standardized tests and achieve higher levels of education, such as graduating from high school and college, than students from lower-SES families. Across many research studies, the relationship between SES status and academic achievement has been consistent and strong (Sirin 2005). Although there are certainly individual exceptions, the larger trends indicate a long-standing and persistent achievement gap between minority and poor students and their more advantaged peers white (Lee 2002).

Furthermore, families with similar SES levels tend to congregate in the same neighborhoods such that students living in the same zip code are often segregated by both race/ethnicity and SES. Particularly in urban areas, large neighborhoods have a high concentration of low-SES minority students where the negative relationship between SES and academic outcomes is exacerbated because the community lacks resources and there are fewer options for students to improve their conditions.

In education, one common goal among all stakeholder groups is to break the relationship between school quality and student zip code by increasing the number and availability of high-quality schools in low-SES neighborhoods. Different stakeholder groups may disagree on the means to achieve this goal, yet all education stakeholder groups, proponents and opponents of school choice alike, aspire to achieve it. School choice advocates regard policies such as open enrollment, charter schools, vouchers, and ESA programs as effective means to close the achievement gap between minority and low-income students and their peers by increasing the number and availability of high-quality schools in low-SES neighborhoods. Thus, school choice advocates frame access to increased high-quality schooling options as a civil rights issue.

Although opponents agree that closing the achievement gap is a critical public policy issue, they maintain that school choice does not live up to its promise to improve educational conditions for minority and low-income students, a topic taken up in more detail in the next chapter. While school choice has received a positive response from civil rights organizations, this endorsement is a shifting proposition based on how policies play out in practice. For example, in 2016, the National Association for the Advancement of Colored People (NAACP), a civil rights organization dedicated to the elimination of race-based discrimination, issued a resolution calling for a moratorium on charter school expansion until such time that charter schools are subjected to the same transparency and accountability as traditional public schools, public funds are not diverted to charter schools at the expense of traditional public schools, charter schools cease to segregate the highest-performing children, and charter schools no longer expel students whom traditional public schools then have a duty to educate (National Association for the Advancement of Colored People 2016).

In advance of a discussion of the research evidence on school choice in chapter 3, it is important to point out the theory of action behind the argument that school choice can improve educational conditions in communities with traditionally underperforming schools. School choice advocates invoke two mechanisms to break the relationship between school quality and zip code. First, they argue that school choice policies will encourage more high-quality schools, namely, charter and private schools, to open in low-SES neighborhoods. Second, they argue that school choice policies allow students living in low-SES neighborhoods to avail themselves of more high-quality schools by having access to high-quality schools outside their neighborhood, including high-quality public and private schools. I discuss the outcomes of both theories of action in the following chapter.

In the contemporary school choice environment, it is also necessary to broaden the perspective of who chooses schools. Based on history, the prognostications held that school choice policies would further segregate public education through the exit of white students, leaving district schools with disproportionate numbers of minority students. These projections were based on the outcomes of earlier school choice policies, specifically freedom-of-choice plans and the reactions of white families to desegregation policies, where white students were the primary actors in school choice policies. The current school choice landscape, however, is more complex and requires an expanded perspective of school choice actors. White students are not the only group to avail themselves of school choice options. Rather, substantial numbers of minority students are participating in school choice, and their actions hold the same potential to lead to segregated school conditions as the actions of white students. Thus, all students who participate in school choice, regardless of race, may enter schools that were more or less racially segregated than the schools they exited. In some cases, segregated school conditions can be more attributable to minority students' self-segregating in schools of choice rather than white students leaving their minority peers behind.

Conclusion

This chapter has discussed the major arguments that support school choice policies within the context of education reform. As an instrument of education reform, school choice policies have risen to address problems with the public school system. The arguments and counterarguments associated with choice were presented, stripped of the political rhetoric as readers would encounter them in the public discourse, in order to understand and evaluate these arguments on their own accord.

In the next chapter, I examine the research evidence to evaluate the extent to which school choice policies have lived up to the aspirations and outcomes that proponents argued would arise from these policies.

THE RESEARCH EVIDENCE

In this chapter, I examine the research on school choice policies. The chapter is organized by the major questions associated with school choice polices, followed by a discussion of the research that has addressed each question.

The most difficult and controversial decision in presenting the research on a politically charged issue like school choice is to determine what counts as research. The answer to this decision dictates what reports, articles, and books are included in the discussion and which are not. There are also many sources of information on school choice from think tanks, universities, advocacy groups, and others that advocate both for and against school choice policies. This chapter includes research from all of these sources, but it is important to note that not everything they publish is considered research for the purpose of this chapter.

For our purposes, "research" refers to empirical studies that collect and analyze data. The data can be primary sources, meaning that the authors collected the data in the course of conducting research, or secondary sources, meaning the authors analyzed or reanalyzed data that others collected. Empirical studies collect both quantitative data, which are measured, recorded, and analyzed numerically, and qualitative data, which are measured, recorded, and analyzed through other formats, such as interviews and observations. The most common data sources used in school choice research are academic achievement indicators such as standardized test scores, graduation rates, dropout rates, and college aptitude tests like the Scholastic Aptitude Test and the American College Test. Data are also collected through student attendance records, government reports, interviews, focus groups, and surveys. The most informative research for our purposes comes from methods that create comparison groups to account for differences between choosers and nonchoosers. Meta-analyses, a statistical technique to synthesize the results across several individual studies, are useful empirical studies to provide a picture of outcomes across several studies conducted in multiple contexts and across many years.

In general, the chapter does not use other types of publications on school choice, such as commentaries, editorials, or policy papers that discuss empirical research.

Although these nonempirical sources of information certainly play an important role to inform and even persuade the public and policymakers about school choice policies, they involve the interpretation of results by a third party rather than an interpretation by the original researchers and are often written in a persuasive rather than informative tone.

I present the research in this chapter in the most comprehensive and unbiased manner that I can possibly accomplish. Thus, the chapter focuses on the results; I will not come to a conclusion on how the research should guide the policy decisions. There are instances, however, when the bulk of the research points to a decided outcome of school choice. In these cases, a nonbiased review of the research dictates that the discussion is presented in a manner that reflects the weight of the research evidence, regardless if it favors or disfavors school choice policies. In these cases, I devote more text to discussing the outcome that is supported by the bulk of the research evidence rather than presenting an equal amount of counterevidence. In other cases, the results are either mixed or inconclusive. I indicate this fact while presenting research to support both sides.

I summarize the general trends that emerge through a broad reading of the research literature. It is possible that individual examples in a local setting or individual studies counter the general trends I present in this chapter. But to the extent that my treatment of the research is an accurate reflection of the prevalent findings in the academic literature as whole, these contradictory examples will be the exception, not the rule.

Finally, it is important to mention the challenges of conducting research on school choice. To the layperson, the logistics of conducting research may appear cumbersome, the questions too limited in scope to be of practical use, and the outcomes less definitive than one would prefer for the purpose of making policy decisions. However, no single study provides the definitive answer to the big questions about school choice. Rather, the answers are found in the incremental contributions of individual research studies that have each answered a narrow, specific research question. The discussion in this chapter is derived by examining the results across these individual studies. Of course, no study is perfect. All research studies have limitations, and these should be taken into consideration when summarizing or interpreting the results.

The first challenge in conducting research on school choice is comparing choosers and nonchoosers. One cannot simply compare the academic outcomes of students who participate in school choice to those who do not or do a straight comparison of schools of choice to other types of schools. The comparison is more complicated than it appears because choosers are fundamentally different from nonchoosers. To measure school choice outcomes requires separating out the impact of attending a school of choice from the inherent characteristics of the choosers themselves. The basic problem is one of self-selection. Those who voluntarily choose to participate in school choice are likely different from those who do not. Some of the differences are directly observable and measurable. Researchers can measure parental income and education levels, for example, to understand the extent to which students who participate in school choice programs come from wealthier, more educated families than students who do not participate in such programs. But how does one separate the impact of coming from a family with more observed advantages, like higher income and education levels, from the impact of attending a school of choice? Other student characteristics, such as motivation or parents' educational expectations, are intangible and more difficult to measure yet play a powerful role in student academic achievement outcomes. For example, choosers who take the time and energy to learn about and enroll in schools of choice likely differ substantively on these intangible characteristics from nonchoosers.

Most intangible characteristics are measured through self-reported instruments such as surveys, focus groups, and interviews. Methodologically, one limitation of these instruments is that participants may report socially desirable answers rather than reporting candidly. Thus, there can be discrepancies between what participants report and their subsequent actions. In addition, the self-reported nature of these data means that it is extremely difficult to disentangle the web of motivations and influences that factor into school choice decisions. Parents may not be able to articulate, or may not want to articulate, why they selected one school choice option over all other available options.

Second, all the studies reviewed in this chapter are based on social science research methods. The key implication for readers is that the studies are not conducted with the same controls available in experimental research studies like those conducted in laboratory conditions. Rather, school choice programs are ongoing, subject to the uncertainties of the real world, and social science research is conducted in this decidedly messy environment. To begin, it is unethical to deny education resources to students in order to conduct research, so researchers are unable to carry out traditional treatment and control studies. Also, the research process rarely begins at the very beginning of a policy, and the schools under study continue to change well after the research is complete. In some cases, quasi-experimental designs, where the researcher has some control over the research conditions, are possible. And in other instances, research has been conducted under randomized conditions where students are assigned to schools of choice according to chance. The primary advantage of research conducted under randomized conditions is that this approach eliminates differences between participants and nonparticipants at the outset of the research so that subsequent differences in outcomes can be more attributable to school choice policies.

The balance of this chapter is organized by the major questions about school choice that are most relevant to a general audience to understand school choice outcomes. Each question is followed by a discussion of the research evidence to address it.

Have Charter Schools Fostered Innovation and Efficiency?

In general, charter schools have not developed new innovative teaching and learning methods as proponents envisioned. By and large, teaching and learning in charter school classrooms looks similar to teaching and learning in district public school classrooms. The notable exception is that charter schools have implemented some administrative and organizational advancements.

Charter schools have not developed innovative teaching and learning practices for two reasons. First, these schools organize themselves in structures that resemble the public school system, and they have been impacted by the larger, overpowering influence of standardization in public education.

The earliest charter schools, those that opened in the early 1990s when school laws expanded rapidly, were often small and independent. Named "mom-and-pop charter schools" after small, independent, family-run small businesses, the early charter school operators were seeking broad flexibility regarding traditional school district regulations. The first charter schools were started by educators who were seeking relief from the overregulated public school system and wanted to "do things differently, whose educational vision and professional norms have been frustrated by conventional schools and their bureaucracies" (Manno et al. 1998, 540). Many of these educators aspired to realize an alternative vision of education that was not possible in the public school system (US Department of Education 2000). They sought administrative autonomy but also the ability to determine the content of their academic programs, how student learning would be assessed, and how their school would be held accountable, all of which was to be documented in charter contracts.

Over time, however, charter schools have replicated some of the same hierarchical organizational structures in the public school system that they sought to reform (Bulkley 2005). Independent charter schools are giving way to charter management networks that in many ways function much like school districts. Charter management networks are a centralized authority that sets policy for the schools within the network. In 2014–2015, a third of all charter schools were associated with a charter management network (Center for Research on Education Outcomes 2017a), and the percentage of students enrolled in networked charter schools rose from 29 percent in 2005 to 40 percent in 2014 (National Alliance for Public Charter Schools 2017a).

Franchised charter schools are affiliated through a charter school network. Similar to private franchises, they share a common curriculum, a centralized organizational structure, and marketing and advertising strategies. Some of the best-known charter schools are franchised charter schools that are part of a larger network of charter schools. The Knowledge Is Power Program (KIPP) schools are a charter school franchise that has received considerable mainstream attention among policymakers, the media, and researchers. Policymakers have actively recruited KIPP schools to their cities and states. The KIPP national network includes over 200 charter schools. All KIPP schools follow the same educational principles, are organized similarly, can be found on the same website, and implement consistent rules and regulations that govern nearly all aspects of school operations, from student conduct to personnel issues (http://www.kipp.org).

The expansion of charter schools and charter school networks is an intentional outcome of policies intended to replicate successful educational models. Replication is an intentional growth strategy so that successful charter school models scale, allowing as many students as possible to be served by what school choice advocates consider to be proven, quality educational options. Replication has been supported on two fronts: philanthropic organizations have invested in the growth of successful charter schools directly, and national charter school organizations have encouraged state policymakers to pass legislation designed to encourage the replication of successful charter schools through efforts such as streamlining the renewal process for successful schools and finding as many legal mechanisms as possible for successful charter schools to open new sites, such as providing start-up funding. While there are considerable challenges to charter school replication (Center for Research on Education Outcomes 2013), the net result of replication policies is the expansion of existing charter school models rather than investing in local initiatives or incubating new methods of teaching and learning.

Charter schools emerged at the same time as standards-based accountability, another major shift in US public education. In 2001, the federal No Child Left Behind Act ushered in a new era of assessments and accountability provisions that required all schools, including charter schools, to teach to the same academic standards, take the same standardized tests, and be held accountable to student performance on standardized tests through state accountability systems. Standards-based accountability imposed the requirement that charter schools must be evaluated exactly like all other public schools; they must use a consistent procedure and meet the standardized academic outcomes determined at the state level, that is, beyond the purview of individual charter school operators, authorizers, and contracts (US Department of Education 2000).

Standards-based accountability has been criticized for promoting standardization among all schools (Ravitch 2010). Critics say that standardization in public education encourages uniformity in academic practices that leads to the narrowing of the academic curriculum and consistency in classroom practices from school to school (McNeil 2000). Standardization, they say, is a threat to the sustainability of schools with innovative missions and educational programs because the visionary culture of innovative schools eventually will succumb to the conformity of standardization (Giles and Hargreaves 2006). Researchers warned against the potential of standardization to compromise charter school innovations:

> The pairing of charter schools with accountability obscures the disciplinary nature inherent in this arrangement. Primarily, the pairing of accountability with charter schools hides the conformity required in the curriculum to meet testing demands while

Standardization,
they say, is a threat
to the sustainability
of schools with
innovative missions and
educational programs
because the visionary
culture of innovative
schools eventually
will succumb to
the conformity of
standardization.

implying that schools are free to teach as they see fit. (Opfer 2001, 209)

Thus, a major reason that charter schools have not developed innovative teaching and learning practices is that they lack the autonomy to determine student academic outcomes and define how charter schools are held accountable. Of the four major components of school autonomy (finance, personnel, curriculum and instruction, and academic outcomes), charter schools have the most autonomy in the areas of finance and personnel, and that is where they have instituted some innovative practices (Finnigan 2007).

The lack of autonomy to determine student academic outcomes and little to no flexibility for charter schools to diversify school accountability requirements have effectively curtailed the development of the innovative schools and instructional practices that school choice proponents expected. Standards-based accountability created pressures for charter schools to implement instructional practices that are similar to those implemented by district public schools.

As a result, charter schools have not fostered pedagogical Innovations (emphasis on the capital "I") as school choice proponents envisioned, meaning innovations that had never existed before (Lake 2008). Instead, they have implemented innovations (emphasis on the lowercase "i") that exist elsewhere but may be novel for the community in which the charter school is located (Lubienski 2003). For example, a charter school may open that focuses on the arts or on a nationally recognized reading program. Presumably both schools opened due to demand for these educational approaches in the local community. The idea of an arts school alone is not innovative, of course, since arts schools have existed for many years. It's also more than likely that charter schools do not develop new pedagogical programs. Rather, what is more likely is that the charter school is using a recognized reading program that is used in other schools in other communities, including district public schools. For the parents and students of the local community, however, an arts charter school or a charter school based on the recognized reading program is an innovative choice.

Much research has looked into the black box of charter school operations at the school level for lessons that can be applied to other educational settings and schools (Fuller 2000; Berends et al. 2010), but it has not uncovered novel practices. Rather, charter schools have intentionally embraced and implemented some best practices found in other schools but have done so in an intensive manner that influences school operations. For example, successful charter schools are characterized by an emphasis on high academic expectations for all students, data-driven instruction, and individualized student attention. such as tutoring and longer school days (Fryer 2014). The impact of these existing practices is intensified by another unique characteristic of charter schools: they are often considerably smaller than district public schools, particularly at the high school level. In general, smaller schools are less hierarchical than larger schools, meaning less distance between teachers and administrators, which facilitates the implementation of school policies.

Who Chooses? What Is the Impact on the Segregation of Students by Race/Ethnicity and the Stratification of Students by Social Class?

The roots of school choice policies have been inextricably tied to desegregation since southern school districts employed freedom-of-choice plans in response to *Brown v. Board of Education*. The relationship between school choice policies and school segregation thus persists as a critical public policy question. In most cases, school choice policies further separate students who are already separated in the public school system through segregation along racial lines, stratified by socioeconomic status, or sorted by academic ability. The separation of students by race/ethnicity and socioeconomic status is particularly acute under open, unregulated, or market-based school policies.

In most cases, school choice policies further separate students who are already separated in the public school system through segregation along racial lines, stratified by socioeconomic status, or sorted by academic ability.

In locations where school choice policies include specific provisions to promote integration, schools have experienced some degree of desegregation and integration.

To provide sufficient context to understand the impact of school choice policies, understanding two larger trends that influence school segregation is key. First, the US public school population has become considerably more diverse since the civil rights movement. From 1968 to 2011, white student enrollment in US schools declined 28 percent, black student enrollment increased 19 percent, and Latino student enrollment increased 495 percent (Orfield et al. 2014). For this reason, while the public discourse on desegregation following *Brown* was largely focused on segregated conditions for white and black students in the southern and eastern parts of the United States, the current racial composition of the US public school system mandates including Latino students in any analyses of school choice outcomes. Second, many US families live in neighborhoods that are separated by both race/ethnicity and socioeconomic status. Essentially, many families congregate in neighborhoods with other families that are similar to themselves, and it stands to reason that schools would reflect the segregated conditions that are present in the neighborhoods in which they are located. Therefore, the most appropriate benchmark to assess segregation is the extent to which the student body composition of schools of choice reflects the demographics of their local neighborhood.

In the years following *Brown*, there was substantial progress in school desegregation from the 1960s through the 1980s. Since that time, however, schools in the southern United States have regressed with respect to segregation, and now, more than sixty years after *Brown*, southern schools are as segregated as they were in 1967, at the height of the civil rights movement. Interestingly, however, blacks in the South attend less segregated schools than their peers in other parts of the United States because the segregation of black students is more pronounced in large metropolitan areas. Latino students, the largest and fastest-growing student racial/ethnic group in the United States in the decades since *Brown*, have experienced high levels of segregation, particularly in western states where Latino student enrollments are highest.

In 2011, students from all racial groups were more likely to attend schools with higher percentages of students from their own racial/ethnic group, and this was particularly so of white students. The typical white student attended a school whose student body composition was 73 percent white, 8 percent black, and 12 percent Latino. The typical black student attended a school that was 49 percent black, 28 percent white, and 17 percent Latino. And the typical Latino student attended a school that was

57 percent Latino, 25 percent white, and 11 percent black (Orfield et al. 2014).

With respect to school choice, private schools enroll more white and affluent students than district public schools do. In forty-three states, white students are over-represented in private schools, and private schools in the South were the most segregated, enrolling high percentages of white students relative to district public schools (Southern Education Foundation 2016). Segregated conditions in private schools are largely the result of socioeconomic differences between white and minority students, where white families are more likely to have sufficient resources to pay private school tuition.

The most informative research on the relationship between segregation and school choice has been conducted in charter schools. Whereas tuition costs limit the availability of private schools to the general population, charter schools are free public schools and are available to a much broader cross-section of the student population than private schools are. In some states, such as Arizona, where charter schools enroll a substantial percentage of the student population, the broad availability of charter schools provides the best indication of what to expect under a large-scale, market-based school choice policy environment. Also, charter schools emerged at the same time as the emergence of large-scale databases, allowing for informative studies that compare charter and district public schools located in the same geographic area or track student attendance patterns as they enter and exit schools. These studies go beyond overall comparisons of the charter and district public student populations to capture the outcomes of school choice decisions and changes in student enrollment at the school level.

Historically, the lens by which to evaluate segregation and school choice has been to examine the school attendance patterns of white students, who were more likely to "choose" schools by moving to a new neighborhood, a phenomenon known as white flight. Overall, the research evidence indicates that in school choice environments, white students are more likely to attend schools with more white students. These patterns are consistent with the previous white flight trends. These trends are not evident in straightforward comparisons of the student demographics of district public and charter schools. In overall demographic comparisons, a lower percentage of white students are enrolled in charter schools than in district public schools. In 2014, 34 percent of charter school students were white compared to district public schools, which enrolled 51 percent white students. Minority students are overrepresented in charter schools, where 27 percent of students were black and 31 percent Latino compared to district public schools, which enrolled 15 percent black students and 25 percent Hispanic students (National Center for Education Statistics 2015, table 216.30).

Yet patterns of white flight emerge when student demographics are compared between charter and district public schools that are located near each other or student attendance patterns are tracked as they exit and enter schools. These more advanced methodological approaches are intended to capture student enrollment patterns (Renzulli and Evans 2005; Cobb and Glass 1999).

Student attendance patterns in charter schools, however, are more complex than the white flight seen in the years immediately following *Brown*. In addition to the congregation of white students in schools of choice, minority students are self-segregating into charter schools with other minority students, a phenomenon that exacerbates segregated conditions in charter schools. US public schools, I have noted, are generally segregated by race/ethnicity. Yet when minority students leave segregated district public schools, they attend more segregated charter schools. These trends were evident among black and Native American students, both of whom entered charter schools with higher percentages of black and Native American students, respectively, than the district public schools they exited. Latinos are the only student group that does not consistently self-segregate with other Latino students in charter schools (Garcia 2008). Self-segregation is a potential reason why 48 percent of charter schools are majority-minority schools, enrolling more than 50 percent black or Latino students compared to only 25 percent of district public schools that enroll majority-minority student populations (National Center for Education Statistics 2017c).

It is difficult to derive conclusions about the stratification of students in charter schools by socioeconomic status because up to 30 percent of charter schools do not report data on students who qualify for the federal free and reduced-price lunch, the most common metric of poverty status (Frankenberg, Siegel-Hawley, and Wang 2010; Center for Education Reform 2014). According to schools with data available, 36 percent of charter schools are considered high-poverty schools, defined as enrolling more than 75 percent of students who qualify for the federal free and reduced-price lunch program compared to 25 percent of district public schools (National Center for Education Statistics 2017c).

How Do the Outcomes of School Choosers Compare to Those of Nonchoosers?

The question of how the academic achievement outcomes of schools of choice compare to district public schools is one of the most pressing in education. Policymakers and advocates on both sides of the debate who are looking for a clear winner, however, are often disappointed with the results. There are no simple, clear answers to guide education policy going forward. Nonetheless, there is some historical evidence to understand the academic outcomes one would expect under different types of school choice policies.

Of the various types of school choice, there is substantial research evidence on only three types: private schools, vouchers, and charter schools. Home-schooled students are excluded from state educational requirements, so there are few to no data available to compare the academic achievement of home-schooled students to students in other educational settings. Likewise, most states do not track open enrollment students who live in one school district and attend school in a different district. Education savings accounts (ESAs) are the most recent type of school choice, and the lack of accountability requirements means that there are few to no data available on the academic performance of students participating in an ESA program.

Private Schools

In general, private school students score higher on standardized achievement tests and college entrance exams and achieve higher college attendance and completion rates than public school students (Center on Education Policy 2007). Drawing conclusions from the research on private schools is tenuous, however, because these schools enroll a more advantaged student population in general than both district public and charter schools do. Therefore, while the academic outcomes of private schools exceed those of other types of schools, it is difficult to assess the extent to which the outcomes are a result of a private school education or the individual and socioeconomic advantages of students attending the schools.

To compare the academic achievement of private schools to other schools, researchers have employed sophisticated statistical models to separate the academic achievement attributable to student characteristics from the academic achievement gains attributable to private schools. These statistical models are intended to put private schools and public schools on a level playing field with respect to student background characteristics before comparing the academic outcomes. This research indicates that after accounting for the home environment advantages of private school students, the academic achievement of public school students is higher than that of private school students (Lubienski and Lubienski 2014).

There is also evidence that public schools are gaining ground on private schools, at least on standardized tests. Researchers attribute the gains to pressures associated with high-stakes accountability policies. For example, when No Child Left Behind was implemented in 2000, private schools scored 14 points higher than public schools on average in fourth-grade reading on the National Assessment of Educational Progress, a longitudinal academic assessment. By 2013, the private school advantage was reduced to 5 points on average (Wong, Cook, and Steiner 2015).

Charter Schools

The academic achievement of charter schools is mixed. Some charter schools perform well compared to district public schools, many perform about the same as district public schools, and others underperform relative to district public schools.

In general, studies indicate that charter schools outperform district public schools as measured by standardized test scores, but the charter school advantage is modest and the positive outcomes are inconsistent across all subject areas. In most studies, charter school achievement is stronger in mathematics than reading, a trend that is yet to be explained with sufficient detail (Jeynes 2012). For example, the magnitude and direction of the results from a 2014 meta-analysis are typical of the results found in other studies of charter schools. Charter schools made greater academic gains than district public schools in mathematics but not reading. The results across all grade levels were generally positive but modest. In mathematics, the estimated effect of attending a charter school for one year, as opposed to a district public school, was a statistically significant 1.4 percentile points. In reading, the estimated effect of attending a charter school for one

In general, studies indicate that charter schools outperform district public schools as measured by standardized test scores, but the charter school advantage is modest and the positive outcomes are inconsistent across all subject areas.

year was 0.6 percentile points, not statistically significant (Betts and Tang 2014).

The academic achievement results, however, are not strong enough to conclude that charter schools outperform district public schools as a whole. In fact, this either-or question has not proven informative to researchers. As a result, this basic question is rarely addressed as the sole focus of rigorous research on charter schools. Rather, researchers recognize the tremendous diversity of individual charter schools within the charter school sector. The most informative research indicates that the type of charter school matters. Three types of charter schools stand out in the research: online schools, no-excuses schools, and the age and start-up status of charter schools.

Online education providers have leveraged the flexibility of charter school laws and technological advances to create a growing segment of schools that allow students to complete educational requirements using the Internet. The most comprehensive research on the academic growth of students attending online charter schools indicates that these students are substantially underperforming compared to students who attend physical district public schools. On average, the underperformance of online charter school students compared to students attending a physical district public school was equivalent to the loss of a full academic year of instruction in mathematics and half an academic year in reading. The academic losses were greater for minority, low-income, special education students, and English language learners. Also, the mobility rate for online charter school students was considerably higher. Online charter school students changed schools at a rate two to three times higher than their peers in physical district public schools. Finally, specific policies and practices of online schools are associated with both positive and negative student academic achievement outcomes. For example, self-paced classes are associated with higher academic achievement outcomes for both mathematics and reading across all grade levels except high school mathematics. On the other hand, unmonitored online interactions and the expectation that parents actively participate in instruction are both associated with lower student outcomes (Center for Research on Education Outcomes 2015).

No-excuses schools are another type of educational approach that has taken hold in the charter school sector. These schools, which are mostly located in urban areas and serve minority students, particularly black students, are characterized by conspicuously high academic expectations, embracing a college-going culture, additional instructional time, and a heavy emphasis on standardized test scores to drive decision making. Some of the most recognizable charter schools that employ instructional methods consistent with the no-excuses approach are associated with charter school networks such as Knowledge

Is Power Program (KIPP), YES Prep, Uncommon Schools, and Aspire charter schools (Macey, Decker, and Eckes 2009). These schools are controversial for demanding working conditions that lead to high teacher and student turnover rates (Yeh 2013). In a review across many individual studies, no-excuses charter schools were associated with positive academic achievement gains compared to similar students attending district public schools. On average, black students who attended a no-excuses charter school for one year closed the achievement gap with their white peers by 25 percent in mathematics and 20 percent in reading (Cheng et al. 2017).

The age and the start-up status of the charter school are other important factors related to academic outcomes. There is consistent evidence that new charter schools score lower than more established charter and district public schools. The academic outcomes of new charter schools increase over time, however, and after approximately five years in operation there are no discernible differences in achievement between new charter schools and comparable public schools (Sass 2006; Carruthers 2012). The start-up status of the charter school is also related to academic outcomes. Converted charter schools—those that were operational as a district public school or private school prior to becoming a charter school—are less likely to have lower test scores during the first years in operation. New start-ups, defined as schools that are beginning operations for the first time, are more likely to have lower scores in the initial years (Center for Research on Education Outcomes 2013).

Another charge against charter schools is that they would further sort public schools by academic achievement where students of similar academic ability would congregate in the same schools. Several components of this argument deserve separate treatment. The first charge is that charter schools would cream-skim the most academically talented students, leaving low-performing students in district public schools. Although there are thematic charter schools that attract students of similar academic ability, programs in district public schools also result in the sorting of students by academic ability. In other words, the sorting of students by academic ability is evident in both charter and district public schools. For example, some high-profile charter schools, such as the BASIS network of schools, advertise a rigorous academic experience and have been nationally recognized for high academic outcomes. It stands to logic that these schools are likely to cream-skim academically talented students by the very nature that only high-achieving students may apply for admission. In addition, many alternative charter schools attract low-performing students who have experienced academic challenges in other school settings. Similarly, district public schools also operate academically advanced programs and schools for high-achieving students and alternative programs and schools for struggling students. The bulk of the research evidence indicates that charter schools have not engaged in wholesale cream-skimming, defined as attracting and enrolling the most talented students. Moreover, students who exit district public schools to enroll in a charter school are often behind their peers academically (Garcia 2008).

The second charge is that charter schools would enroll lower percentages of special education students because they are more costly to educate. Special education students require additional academic supports to be successful, and these supports can be costly, particularly for students with severe disabilities such as visual and physical impairments (Lacireno-Paquet et al. 2002). Overall, charter schools enroll lower percentages of special education students compared to district public schools. Special education students accounted for 8 percent of student enrollment in charter schools compared to 13 percent of district public schools (Center for Research on Education Outcomes 2013). Lower special education enrollment in charter schools may be the result of either special education parents not choosing charter schools for their children or charter schools dissuading special education students from enrolling.

It is important to point out that the sorting of students by school represents only a small part of how students are grouped by ability. Most of the stratification by academic ability happens within schools where students are grouped in different classes or tracks based on academic ability. Both charter schools and district public schools group students by ability level. There is little to no academic evidence to indicate that charter schools are more or less likely to group in this way.

Finally, readers should be aware of the education reforms occurring in New Orleans. After Hurricane Katrina destroyed much of the city in 2005, including nearly all public schools, reformers seized the opportunity to replace district public schools with charter schools, creating the most concentrated market-based educational system in the country. The New Orleans public school system is one of a kind: all schools are either charter schools or have applied for charter school status. This swift and dramatic shift of the city's educational landscape has drawn national attention. Initial research evidence indicates that post-Katrina, student performance on standardized test scores has increased in the all-charter school system compared to results before the storm (Harris and Larsen 2016). With respect to segregation, New Orleans schools were highly segregated prior to the storm, and with the education reforms that followed, it remains segregated by race and stratified by income (Weixler, Barrett, and Jennings 2017). In addition to outcomes, many academics have studied New Orleans to understand how governance structures, school operations, and policies have shifted under market-based reforms (https://educationresearchalliancenola.org).

Vouchers

Similar to the outcomes of other school choice policies, the academic achievement results for school vouchers are mixed. The research indicates positive results in some cities and in some subject areas and negative results in other locations. In general, there is no evidence that vouchers are associated with significant and sustained improvement in student test scores. Yet the overall conclusions about the impact of vouchers are challenged by the fact that the existing voucher programs are scattered throughout a few states and cities, that all are structured differently, and that they are targeted toward specific student populations, such as low-income or special education students. There is no voucher program in the United States that resembles Friedman's seminal voucher proposal to assess the outcomes of a universal school voucher program.

In addition, the research evidence can seem contradictory: a study at one point in time may be contradicted by researchers examining the same data using a different method, or new research evidence may become available that is contrary to older research evidence. One reason for the seemingly contradictory evidence on school vouchers is that the results are not robust, meaning that any positive (or negative) conclusions may not hold up consistently in different locations, across different research methods, and at different times. For example, vouchers have produced positive results in some subject areas in New York and Washington, DC (Hoxby, Murarka, and Kang 2009). The results, however, are modest, inconsistent, or isolated to one subject, either reading or mathematics (Wolf et al. 2013). In addition, research on voucher programs in Louisiana and Indiana indicates that students who participated in these programs scored lower than their peers in district public schools (Mills and Wolf 2016).

Given the politically charged environment, I turn to the research evidence and conclusions on school vouchers from the perspective of an organization that is favorable to them. EdChoice, a school choice advocacy organization, conducted a review of the research on vouchers from 1998 to 2016 in Louisiana, New York City, Charlotte, Toledo, Dayton, Milwaukee, and Washington, DC. It accepted eighteen studies that met its criteria of rigorous research. Of these studies, its analysts concluded that fourteen showed some positive results for vouchers, but only six of those fourteen studies indicated that vouchers resulted in positive results for all students; the remaining eight studies provided evidence of positive results for only a subset of students. Two studies indicated negative results, both from Indiana, and two indicated that vouchers were not associated with any visible effect on student achievement (Forster 2016).

School choice proponents often charge that negative results are due to flaws in the design of school voucher programs, arguing that only a universal school choice program is capable of delivering dramatic improvements in student achievement. Other researchers have reviewed the same body of evidence and reached similar conclusions: the impact of school vouchers is modest at best. They argue that the lackluster evidence associated with school vouchers is insufficient to merit expansion to a universal program. They also point out that the political popularity of school vouchers is distracting policymakers from focusing on other policies with more consistent, proven evidence of improving student achievement such as teacher training and early child education programs (Carnoy 2017).

The Milwaukee voucher program is a special case because it is the longest-running such program in the United States, has been the subject of the most research, and has provided the most informative longitudinal evidence on the impact of vouchers. A comprehensive research program in 2012 involving thirty-one reports over five years reached the modest conclusion about school vouchers in Milwaukee that they were not harmful but falls short of claiming that they have been positive overall:

> Our research revealed a pattern of school choice results that range from neutral (no significant differences between Choice and MPS) to positive (clear benefit to Choice). Although we examined virtually every possible way that school choice could systematically impact people, schools, and

neighborhoods in Milwaukee, we have found no evidence of any harmful effects of choice. (Wolf 2012, 4)

Finally, the relationship between vouchers and other academic achievement indicators, such as graduation rates and postsecondary attendance, is more positive and consistent. There is evidence that students who participate in vouchers are more likely to graduate from high school and attend college at higher rates (Chingos and Peterson 2013). These positive academic outcomes have been found in voucher programs in different locations. Students in private schools may benefit from the college-going culture of private schools and the personal benefits associated with exposure to families with substantial social and educational capital.

Does the Rising Tide Lift All Boats? What Are the Spillover Effects of School Choice Policies to District Public Schools, and What Are the Implications for Education Reform?

One promise of school choice is that competition will lead to positive outcomes not only for choosers, students who enroll in schools of choice, but also for nonchoosers because district public schools are expected to respond to competitive pressures by improving educational service delivery.

The research evidence indicates that when faced with a competitive environment, school districts responded by opening new schools or initiating new educational programs. Moreover, these new educational offerings were often based on the same or a similar educational philosophy or academic theme as that of neighboring charter schools. This strategy was targeted toward recapturing or stabilizing student enrollment counts by responding to the reasons that parents enrolled their student in a different school. School districts also invested in public relations activities such as advertising programs to promote their educational offerings to prospective parents and parental satisfaction surveys modeled after customer satisfactions surveys found in the private sector. District public school administrators, however, do not look to charter schools as sources of pedagogical innovation (Rofes 1998; Teske, Schneider, Buckley, and Clark 2000).

The more central issue to test the arguments in favor of school choice is the extent to which student academic achievement scores increase in district public schools that operate in a competitive school choice environment. This is a complex question to address through research because the improvement of district public schools is a secondary outcome of school choice policies (see Strauss 2017 as an example). While there is some evidence of academic

The research evidence indicates that when faced with a competitive environment, school districts responded by opening new schools or initiating new educational programs.

outcomes and efficiency gains as a result of competition in general (Belfield and Levin 2002), there is also mixed or non-significant evidence on whether or not competition from charter schools improves outcomes or increases efficiency in public schools in the same locality (Ni 2009).

How Do Parents Make School Choice Decisions?

Under school choice programs, parents serve a key role as education consumers. School choice theories are predicated on the assumption that parent consumers will make logical, rational school choice decisions based on gaining access to the best possible education for their student. Parents are expected to leave low-performing schools in favor of higher-performing schools, which imposes pressure on low-performing schools to improve or close as student enrollment counts fall. These actions are instrumental to generating the appropriate market signals so that all schools respond to school choice in a manner that improves educational conditions. For this reason, how parents make school choice decisions is a key question in order to understand the extent to which these decisions are consistent or inconsistent with the theories of consumer behavior that undergird school choice policies.

Two general methods are used to research parental school choice decisions. The first is to ask parents directly about their school choice decisions. These studies are based on surveys, interviews, and focus groups with parents where they self-report the factors and conditions surrounding their school choice decisions. The second method is to use more indirect methods to capture the results of school choice decisions. These methods involve tracking student attendance behaviors in school choice environments using strategies such as mapping student attendance patterns (based on the assumption that student attendance is the result of a school choice decision) and artifacts of the school choice process, like monitoring the search activity of parents on school choice websites.

A common finding from these methods is that parental actions often contradict their words. Parents self-report that school-level academic achievement is a major influence in their school choice decisions and comment that the socioeconomic and racial/ethnic composition of the student body is not a major factor (Weiher and Tedin 2002). While there is evidence that parents choose schools with higher academic outcomes, there is also a strong pattern that students from almost all racial/ethnic backgrounds are more likely to attend a school their parents choose with relatively high percentages of students from the same racial/ethnic group (Garcia 2008).

The student body composition of schools is an important factor in school choice decisions. For example, when parents search for school information, they prioritize student demographics, such as the racial/ethnic composition of the school, over academic information like test scores (Schneider and Buckley 2002). Also, it is not uncommon for students to exit higher-performing schools to enter lower-performing schools composed of students from the same racial/ethnic background. While parents rate integration and diversity as valuable school characteristics, the schools that minority parents consider enrolling their student in are often composed of high percentages of minority students, and, similarly, the set of schools that white parents consider for enrollment are composed of relatively high percentages of white students.

Research on the choice process is helpful in understanding the reasons behind school choice decisions. White parents indicate that they are conscious of segregated school conditions when making these decisions, but they are conflicted because they want their student to have access to the best school available despite the lack of diversity (Roda and Wells 2013). Others have found that given the strong association between school quality and neighborhood characteristics, the schools that poor and minority parents in low-income neighborhoods have available to them are likely to be segregated and lower performing (Bell 2009).

Also, parents rely heavily on informal sources of information in school choice decisions. Middle-class and white parents, in particular, turn to social networks and online resources to troubleshoot school-related issues and acquire information to make school choice decisions. Families from higher socioeconomic backgrounds can rely on social networks composed of substantial social and educational capital to guide their school choice decisions. There are indications that lower-income and minority parents do not access online information to the same extent as white middle-class parents do and that the social and educational capital in their networks is more limited.

School characteristics other than academic achievement also play an instrumental role in school choice decisions. Parents consider practical issues, such as student well-being, school safety, the availability of transportation to and from school, and the existence of before- and after-school programs, in school choice decisions. These school characteristics are foundational considerations because students are unable to benefit from academic programs unless their basic needs are met. Parents try to determine if their student will feel safe in a school and they feel that they belong there. Or they determine if their student has a reliable means of transportation to get to and from school so they can attend on a regular basis.

The research on how parents choose schools is helpful for evaluating the theory of change behind school choice policies. To the extent that parents make school choice decisions based on race/ethnicity considerations, there is little that most schools can do to improve and respond to parental demands. In addition, given that parents make choices based on practical considerations, such as transportation and the availability of before- and after-school programs, it's logical that schools would implement and advertise these programs to attract and retain students. While school choice proponents have pointed to the potential of school choice to improve and innovate teaching and learning in the classroom, parents do not rely exclusively on such formal information about schools to make decisions. Finally, many school choice proponents point out that the school information available to parents is imperfect, and they argue that accessible and understandable school information is essential to influence parental school choice behaviors that prompt school improvement.

With respect to the results of school choice decisions, there is evidence that parents who avail themselves of school choice policies are highly satisfied with their decision. One consistent research finding is that charter school parents report higher levels of satisfaction with their school than district public school parents do (Barrows, Peterson, and West 2017). School choice proponents often point to high parent satisfaction ratings as an indication that charter schools are responding to parental preferences.

What Are the Financial Impacts of School Choice Policies for Different Stakeholders?

Public education in the United States is primarily a state and local responsibility, and the funding for public education reflects this priority. District public schools are funded from three primary sources: state (46 percent), local (45 percent), and federal (9 percent) (US Census Bureau 2015). Federal dollars represent the smallest portion of school funding and are allotted to states to support targeted programs advanced by the federal government. The bulk of funding for public education comes from state and local sources. Each state allots a specific amount per pupil, and that amount is determined by elected policymakers in each state. In addition, public school districts can access local funds through the passage of bonds and overrides approved by voters in a local election. Charter schools that are not associated with a school district are not able to raise local funds and are funded primarily through state sources.

States also support school choice programs through tax credits that allow individuals and corporations to direct a portion of their tax dollars to private schools. While tax deductions are available to taxpayers to support eligible nonprofit organizations, including churches and private schools, tax credits have a more direct impact on public funds. A deduction reduces the amount of income that is subject to taxes. A tax credit reduces the amount of taxes that either individuals or corporations have to pay. Under tax credit programs, individuals and corporations can direct a portion of their taxes to private schools or organizations that provide scholarships to private schools and receive a dollar-for-dollar reduction in their tax liability. States set the amount of money that individuals and corporations can direct to private schools through tax credits. Each dollar that is directed to private schools under tax credits results in a net loss to the state general fund, reducing the amount of money available to fund public education (Welner 2008, 2017).

School district and charter school budgets are based on student enrollment counts. School choice policies have the most impact on state-level funding because it is a large funding source and the most sensitive to changes in student enrollment counts. The tight association between student enrollment counts and the amount of funding available at the school level is a critical element of school choice policies. The motivating force behind competitive school choice policies is that high-quality schools are expected to attract more students and receive more funding than lower-quality schools, while the inverse relationship should also hold true.

School choice decisions have financial implications because school funding is based on per-pupil formulas where money follows the student. Prior to the implementation of school choice policies, nearly all public funds for education remained within the public school system. Thus, the most controversial school choice policies are those that shift funding away from public schools. For example, charter school policies transfer funding from district public schools to independent organizations outside the public school system, and vouchers and ESAs transfer funds from both district public and charter schools to private institutions and providers. Under open enrollment policies, students move between public schools, and funding shifts between schools within the public school system.

Under voucher programs, the full state-allotted amount per pupil is transferred to private schools, resulting in a loss of revenue for the public school system for each student participating in a voucher program. ESAs, however, are structured differently. Under ESAs, 90 percent of the state-allotted amount per pupil is shifted to private institutions and educational providers, while 10 percent remains in the public school system. Proponents argue that leaving 10 percent of state revenue in state coffers results in a cost savings for the public school system. For example, if a state allotted $5,000 per pupil for education costs, the ESA would be valued at $4,500, which represents the amount available to parents to use to purchase education services for their student. For every student who participates in an ESA program, $500 would remain in the state budget. Proponents argue that the ESA program is a cost savings for states because when students participate in that program, the state does not have to incur the cost associated with educating that student and a portion of the state allotment remains available to spend on public schools. Thus, proponents make the point that all students, including public and charter schools and students, benefit when their peers exit the public school system to participate in an ESA program.

Nevertheless, a number of factors bear on the extent to which schools are able to realize the potential savings. When school choice programs such as ESAs save money at the state level, the result is an increase in the state general fund, which is available to pay for all state services, including funding to all public schools. There are no requirements that policymakers pass the cost savings from school choice programs to public schools. They may allot remaining dollars to other public services or lower taxes, negating any potential fiscal benefits for public schools.

The fiscal impact of charter schools on district public schools is difficult to pinpoint because each state structures charter school funding differently. In general, however, charter schools are primarily funded by state sources. For example, in Arizona, 83 percent of funding for charter schools comes from the state, compared to only 44 percent for district public schools. Given that charter schools are funded primarily through state sources, charter school enrollment counts can have a disproportionate impact on the amount of state dollars available to fund public schools. For this reason, Arizona charter schools enrolled 16 percent of the total student population but accounted for 26 percent of all state general fund expenditures to public education (Arizona Department of Education 2016).

One contentious question is whether charter schools receive less funding than district public schools do. States have adopted different formulas to fund charter schools and address a potential shortcoming in charter school financing because most charter schools lack the authority to levy local taxes through bonds and overrides (Education Commission of the States 2016b). The differences between the funding of charter and district public schools vary widely by state, from a $15 per pupil advantage for charter schools in Tennessee to a $15,600 per pupil disadvantage for charter schools in Louisiana. In 2013, charter schools were funded $3,509 less per pupil on average than district public schools (Batdorff et al. 2014). The straightforward comparison of funding per pupil, however, can be misleading; district public schools may be funded at higher levels because they enroll a higher number of students who are more expensive to educate, such as special education students.

At the state level, the fiscal impact of school choice programs provides a different picture. The key question at the state level is whether school choice programs result in overall cost savings to a state's general fund. Often studies report the cost savings of school choice to "taxpayers." In most cases, reports on the savings to "taxpayers" are essentially cost savings at the state level. According to most studies on the fiscal impact of school choice programs, voucher programs are associated with a neutral impact or cost savings at the state level. These results stand to reason given that the amount allotted for school choice programs, such as vouchers, is equal to the state allotment per pupil. The exact amount of the cost savings differs by individual states. While there is no body of research on the fiscal impact of ESA programs, the fact that the amounts deposited into private savings accounts are less than the state allotment per pupil, one would anticipate that ESA programs result in a net cost savings to the state.

School districts argue, however, that there is a cost implication to vouchers and ESAs because net cost savings at the state level may still result in cost implications at the school district and school level. One major way that schools reduce costs is through taking advantage of economies of scale. Fixed costs such as teacher salaries are reduced through increased enrollment counts. For example, in a class of twenty students, the money available to pay the teacher is equal to the allotment per pupil for twenty students. If two students use a voucher and are no longer enrolled, the public school must still provide a teacher for the remaining eighteen students, yet the funds available for the teacher's salary is reduced by an amount equal to the state allotment for the two students who are participating in the voucher program.

At the student level, it's also important to note the financial disparities of school choice programs. Students participating in vouchers and ESAs receive considerably less public funding than students attending traditional and public schools. Voucher and ESA students receive an amount equivalent to the state allotment per pupil, or less. Students who attend district public school and charter schools, on the other hand, have access to all three sources of public funding: federal, state, and local.

How Has School Choice Been Implemented in Other Countries?

School choice programs have also been implemented in many other countries, including Chile, New Zealand, Sweden, the Netherlands, and Colombia. I will focus on large-scale school choice reforms with broad policy implications. In addition to these large national programs, there are a number of targeted school choice programs in India and Korea, as well as other countries, that I do not discuss here.

Chile has received the most academic attention among international voucher programs. Its universal voucher program, implemented in 1981, is of note because when it began, it was the closest operational version of Friedman's original school voucher proposal. Chilean economic policies, including the school voucher program, were heavily influenced by economists from the University of Chicago, Friedman's intellectual home (Klein 2008). Chile's school voucher program is universal, open to all students, and provides funding to public and private schools based on per-pupil allotments. There is a tight connection between student enrollment counts and the amount of money provided to both public and private schools to educate students. The Chilean voucher program is credited with a dramatic expansion of private schools. In 1990, there were 2,425 private schools in Chile, and by 2010 the number of private schools had more than doubled to 5,545 (Portales and Vasquez Heilig 2014).

A few key changes to the Chilean voucher program are of note because they represent a concerted shift by the government to affect student enrollment patterns through policy rather than relying on market forces. First, when the voucher program began, Chilean private schools could charge students additional fees above and beyond tuition as a requirement of attendance. Student fees were associated with more middle- to higher-income students participating in the voucher program. In 2015, policy changes prohibited private schools from charging additional fees to parents for their child's attendance. Second, private schools were permitted to screen and select students based on their own criteria and some schools used screening policies to shape the composition of their student body by enrolling more advantaged students. Recent policy changes have prohibited student screening in elementary grades, but there are indications that private schools nevertheless continue to charge informal fees to parents because the law is not well enforced. Public schools have always been required to enroll all students. Third, a 2008 policy change allotted additional funding for low-income students, providing new incentives for private schools to enroll low-income students. This policy change is credited with increasing private school enrollments, reducing the percentage of students enrolled in public schools from 42 percent in 2009 to 36 percent in 2016 (Garcia 2017).

Despite Chile's voucher program's implementation in a country with cultural and educational norms different from those in the United States, its results are remarkably similar to the US results. Most research indicates that segregation has increased under Chile's universal voucher program. Middle- and upper-income students are more likely to attend private schools using vouchers, with a higher concentration of low-income students enrolled in Chile's public schools (Portales and Vasquez Heilig 2014). In addition, parents cite academic outcomes as important to their school choice decisions and do not refer to the social composition of the school. Yet, school attendance patterns indicate that student demographics play an influential role in school choice decisions (Schneider, Elacqua, and Buckley 2006).

New Zealand's school choice reforms, known as Tomorrow's Schools, are instructive to education policy discussions because public schools there were transformed swiftly and on a large scale. New Zealanders "threw out the old system in toto, put in a new one, and left fine-tuning until later" (Fiske and Ladd 2000, 12). In 1992, New Zealand implemented a series of reforms similar to charter schools in the United States. Operational control of schools was decentralized from the national authority to local school sites, school attendance zones were abolished and parents were given the right to enroll their student in the school of their choice, competition between schools became a central feature of school improvement efforts, and local educators were afforded considerable autonomy over school operations.

The New Zealand school choice reforms have resulted in increased school segregation and stratification. Wealthier and more-educated families have taken advantage of school choice, and their choices have resulted in the segregation of students by ethnicity and socioeconomic status. Conversely, many low-income families have been unable to participate in the program because they cannot afford the additional costs associated with school choice, such as school fees and transportation (Fiske and Ladd 2000). There are no large-scale data on academic outcomes in New Zealand.

Most researchers point to specific provisions of New Zealand's school choice policies as the reason that Tomorrow's Schools have segregated and stratified public schools. The first is that schools are able to supplement government funding with local fundraising efforts, including noncompulsory fees from parents. Second, when schools reach their enrollment capacity, they are allowed to implement "enrollment schemes" to select students for admission. School fees and enrollment schemes are prevalent in schools with more advantaged student populations: "These enrollment schools have effectively converted a system of 'parent choice' into a system of 'school choice" (Ladd and Fiske 2001, 50). These provisions have created an uneven playing field where the ability for schools to select students has established competitive advantages that allow some schools to attract more advantaged students relative to other schools.

Sweden has also implemented school choice policies, but with provisions that have restricted the scope of reform efforts. Beginning in 1991, select school operations were decentralized from national authority and shifted to the municipal level, where cities acquired the ability to employ teachers. In addition, geographic school boundaries were eliminated through an open enrollment policy that allowed parents to choose any school in their municipal jurisdiction. The impact of the open enrollment policy to influence the student composition of schools was curtailed by allowing geographic distance to serve as a criterion for admission. Thus, while school academic reputation and academic program are strong factors in school choice decisions, geographic factors such as distance, location, and accessibility are also key determinants of student enrollment patterns in Swedish schools (Thelin and Neimosyl 2015). Also, there is evidence of segregation of immigrant and native students and the sorting of students by student background characteristics, but these effects are minimal in Sweden compared to school choice policies in other countries. The percentage of students enrolled in private schools has not increased significantly under school choice policies, hovering around 10 percent both before and after the start of the voucher program (Epple, Romano, and Urquiola 2017).

Analysts point to two provisions of Sweden's school choice policies as potential reasons for limited levels of segregation and sorting. First, oversubscribed schools are required to accept students on a first-come, first-serve basis and are prohibited from selecting students. Second, schools are prohibited from charging additional fees.

Conclusion

Over the past thirty years, an enormous amount of evidence has accumulated about the outcomes of school choice policies. While the evidence does not point to a single clear answer about the effectiveness of these policies, a number of lessons have emerged from research conducted on different types of school choice policies, implemented in different contexts both within and outside the United States. In the final chapter, I present the lessons learned from body of evidence on school choice along with a discussion of what to expect from school choice debates and policies in the future.

FUTURE DIRECTIONS

At the heart of school choice policies is this core question: Who has the authority to determine which schools students can attend? Should the decision be determined by elected officials acting on behalf of their community and administered through government-controlled school systems? Or should parents be allowed to make school choice decisions based on individual interests? This basic decision has prompted a decades-long debate that intersects some of the most fundamental social and political issues in American history. School choice is woven into America's ongoing struggle to desegregate schools and is central to debates about the role of government in society.

School choice decisions are important because education is important. At the family level, parents understand that schooling and schools are influential factors in the academic and life outcomes of their children. On a larger

School choice is woven into America's ongoing struggle to desegregate schools and is central to debates about the role of government in society.

scale, effective public schools are important economic drivers for states and countries, mandating the intense interest of policymakers at every level. The impact of schools, however, extends well beyond the academic lessons in the classroom because schools also influence social norms. For this reason, the government has had an interest in the student body composition of schools to achieve larger social goals, ranging from the Americanization of newly arrived immigrants to desegregation policies intended to combat inequalities and racism.

At the community level, many believe that as public institutions, public schools should be under democratic control with a strong role for government. This perspective favors education policy developed through elected officials (e.g., local school boards) and concerted policies that foster equitable outcomes and opportunities. Market advocates place greater reliance on competition and capitalistic structures to determine the direction of education policy and how schools operate. These entrenched beliefs extend well beyond schools and schooling and are the dividing line between political parties.

The philosophical split is based on whether one views education as a public or a private good. The idea of education as a public good highlights the mutual or collective benefit of education for society as a whole. The argument is that public education provides collective benefits such as fostering an educated citizenry to support a functioning

The idea of education as a public good highlights the mutual or collective benefit of education for society as a whole.

democracy and expanded economic opportunities for all. The challenge is that democratic policies based on collective ideals may at times be at odds with individual preferences, such as when tensions mounted in opposition to busing to desegregate schools. Those who view education as a private good emphasize the individual benefits of education for families and students. They promote policies that encourage families and students to maximize the individual benefits they receive from education by choosing the school that best improves the future prospects of their individual student. In the privatized view of education, collective benefit comes from individuals acting in their own self-interest and schools responding to competitive pressures to increase student enrollments. The tension that arises when education is viewed as a private good is that public education is funded with public tax dollars and individual preferences may run counter to the collective will of the public.

In 2017, school choice was again thrust into the national spotlight by President Donald Trump and his selection of Betsy DeVos as US secretary of education. While Trump had said little about education during the presidential campaign, school choice was the one policy he did trumpet. He chose DeVos, a noted school choice advocate and self-described "disrupter" of the public education status quo, to carry out his agenda. From 2009 to 2016, she was the chairperson for the Alliance for School Choice,

In the privatized view of education, collective benefit comes from individuals acting in their own self-interest and schools responding to competitive pressures to increase student enrollments.

the largest organization in the country promoting school choice programs. In office, President Trump's initial education policy effort is to target $250 million of the $1.4 trillion federal budget to school vouchers for low-income students to attend private religious schools. While the president's school voucher proposal is relatively modest, what is significant about his choice for US secretary of education and the budget allocation is the deliberate shift in federal policy away from its historic emphasis on providing supplemental funding to low-income schools to improve educational delivery for high-need students to providing incentives for low-income families to exit public schools through choice.

President Trump's focus on school choice does not break new ground. Rather, school choice is already entrenched in the political, public, educational, and policy landscapes of American education. Politically, school choice has received bipartisan support from Republicans and Democrats. The underlying reasons for their support may differ, but politicians on both sides of the aisle have found elements of school choice policies that they can champion to advance their education agendas. In broad strokes, Republican policymakers are more likely to advocate for school choice to promote market-based policies, while Democrats are more likely to favor school choice as a means to foster community empowerment. In either case, school choice has remained a key feature of education policy under both Republican and Democratic administrations. For example, President Trump's support for school vouchers was preceded by President Obama's support for charter schools. Race to the Top, President Obama's signature education initiative, required states to promote the expansion of charter schools as a prerequisite for funding. Specifically, states were required to advance school choice by passing a charter school law and removing artificial caps on the number of charter schools (US Department of Education 2009).

Given that the adoption of school choice policies is ultimately political, how the public views school choice is an important factor in policy development because public opinion shapes political discourse and influences which ideas get a hearing and which do not. Polling results are the most common measure of public opinion, although they are not featured as research evidence in this book because polling results can be highly politicized. While they are intended to measure public opinion, they can be used for the more self-serving purpose of shaping public opinion through selective samples and biased survey questions. Also, activists on both sides of the school choice debate have targeted their communication efforts to persuade public opinion to support their favored policies.

In the US context, the Phi Delta Kappa (PDK)/ Gallup survey is the longest-running public opinion poll on education issues. The poll has been administered for almost fifty years and has measured the public's opinion of vouchers twenty time since 1993. Consistently, public support for vouchers has depended on the structure of the survey question. Public support for vouchers is lower when participants are asked if students should be allowed to attend private schools at public expense. When vouchers are framed in this manner, a majority of respondents often oppose school vouchers. When attending a nonpublic school at government expense is portrayed as one of many schooling options, the percentage of respondents favoring school choice is higher, hovering around 50 percent (http://pdkpoll.org).

According to the 2107 PDK survey, 52 percent of Americans oppose vouchers and 39 percent support them based on the question, "Do you favor or oppose allowing students and parents to choose a private school to attend at public expense?" Historically, this version of the question has elicited more negative attitudes toward vouchers than the version that mentions school choice specifically (Rose and Gallup 2002). A more detailed breakdown of the 2017 poll results indicates that nonwhites, lower-income individuals, and Republicans demonstrate stronger support for school vouchers. Also, consistent with the major themes in this book, the degree of public support is dependent on how the voucher proposal is structured. For example, public opinion wanes if the survey question mentions public funding to religious schools specifically, and student participation in a voucher program depends on whether the voucher covers the full cost of tuition (http://pdkpoll.org).

With respect to charter schools, public opinion has been generally favorable and stable over the past decade. For example, *Education Next*, an online journal sponsored by Stanford University and Harvard University, has conducted a public opinion poll on school choice since 2007. The results indicate that the general public regards charter schools very favorably. Over 65 percent of the general public support the formation of charter schools, with higher levels of support among Republicans than Democrats (Peterson, Henderson, West, and Barrows 2017). In 2017, however, support for charter schools dropped precipitously (13 percentage points) (West, Henderson, Peterson, and Barrows 2018). School choice advocates are uncertain if the drop is an aberration or a sign of public discontent with charter schools.

School choice is also embedded in the educational landscape at the local level. In many urban areas, school choice is no longer just the purview of wealthy families. Rather, schools of choice, particularly charter schools, are a common feature in many low-income neighborhoods. As a result, a wider cross-section of families than ever before is participating in school choice. Certainly, many of these families are likely participating in open enrollment or attending a charter schools, rather than private schools, but the explosion of school choice policies over the past two decades means that an entire generation of students has been educated under school choice policies. In these communities, school choice is the norm. Many students who have attended schools of choice are now parents, acting as education consumers and choosing schools for their own children.

Finally, school choice is part of a shift in the overall framework of education policy. In general, education policies have trended toward an economic orientation. School choice is consistent with other education policies that frame educational issues in economic terms. Policymakers have embraced economic perspectives of education policy because economics has the ability to transform what can appear like bewildering social issues into solvable problems. Economists provide legislators with "simple techniques, aids to reasoning" that legislators and their advisors can use to shape the public discourse (Brandl 1985, 387). There are many who are concerned with how economic perspectives, including school choice, commercialize education. Those who wish to advance the more democratic purposes of education argue that framing education in economic terms oversimplifies the full dynamics associated with teaching and learning and the interaction between schools and society. The challenge for those who want to engage in a more holistic discussion of education is that they are forced to discuss the complexities of

Policymakers have embraced economic perspectives of education policy because economics has the ability to transform what can appear like bewildering social issues into solvable problems.

education policies against the more simplistic frameworks that are communicated in market terms and are largely familiar to the general public.

Lessons Learned

School choice policies have also brought to the forefront the question of how and under which conditions research influences education policy. Many believe that sound research should lead the way in policy discussions and that research evidence should be a key instrument in the development and implementation of effective policy solutions. Others point out that academic research can be politicized given with the highly political nature of the school choice debate and it is often used as political ammunition in policy debates (Carnoy et al. 2005). Either way, one should not expect the outcomes of the research evidence alone to win the day and tilt the scale in favor of either side of the school choice debate (Henig 2008, 2009). There is no definitive study, or collection of studies, that one could rely on to make the difficult decisions about whether states, or even countries, should pursue school choice policies.

There are some common lessons learned from the research evidence, however, that readers can use to evaluate the potential outcomes of different school choice proposals. First, school choice policies are more likely to separate, rather than integrate, students from different racial/ethnic and socioeconomic backgrounds. To be clear, the separation of students begins with the residential choice of living in specific neighborhoods. Even before entering school, American students live in neighborhoods that are segregated by race/ethnicity and stratified by income. At a minimum, school choice plans do not reverse segregated neighborhood conditions. Most likely, school choice plans exacerbate the segregation of students by race/ethnicity and the stratification of students by socioeconomic status.

Second, how countries and states structure school choice policies can have a profound impact on how school choice functions at a practical level. In cases where school choice is implemented to complement district public schools, they can be designed as instruments to encourage integration, such as the case with magnet schools. Alternatively, when policies follow market principles and school choice options are viewed as competing with public schools, one can expect similar outcomes in education: some improved efficiency with increased inequities. A logical middle ground is managed competition policies that combine market forces with governmental controls. In managed competition policies, parents are still encouraged to act as consumers to choose the best schools for their children and the pool of education providers is expanded beyond the public school system. But there is a role for government to hold schools accountable, provide transparent information to parents, and enforce laws related to student welfare and safety (Harris 2017).

Third, low-income students face obstacles to participating in school choice plans. In most cases, vouchers do not cover the full cost of attending a private school. When it does not and low-income parents are required to subsidize the voucher in order for their student to attend a private school, one can expect that fewer low-income student will attend these schools. Also, school choice plans do not provide resources to cover the indirect costs of attending a private school, such as transportation. Finally, school choice policies that allow private schools to charge fees present another financial obstacle for low-income students. In cases where private schools are allowed to charge additional fees, higher-income students are in a better financial position to participate in school choice, leading to the stratification of students by income.

Fourth, one should expect student achievement gains under school choice plans to be modest at best and inconsistent across subjects and years. Standardized test results are the most common metric to evaluate education policies, and by this metric, schools of choice do not universally and consistently outperform district public schools. This is a nuanced point, and readers must understand the implications to avoid coming to the false conclusion that school choice policies do not matter. Rather, the more accurate frame is that school choice alone is not an effective driver of education reform. Schools of choice still operate in a larger social context, and this context has a profound influence on student achievement outcomes. Home and community factors are strongly associated with student academic outcomes, relationships that remain robust in all school settings. School choice policies do not alter the impact of nonschool influences on student academic outcomes.

There are other student achievement indicators where the results for schools of choice are positive and more consistent. For example, graduation rates and college entrance rates are generally higher for students who participate in school choice programs. Also, students benefit from the broader exposure and social capital networks that are often available in schools of choice.

Finally, a major reason for the inability of school choice to have an impact on the academic core of schools—teaching and learning—is that school choice came of age at the same time as high-stakes accountability policies that encourage standardization. The result of these broader education policies has been a narrowing of teaching and learning practices. There are limited opportunities for schools of choice to differentiate themselves by diversifying how student achievement is measured, the most influential factor in how teachers teach and student learn. In an age of high-stakes accountability, school performance is measured by how students perform on standardized tests. Standardization means that all schools, including charter schools, are encouraged to be more alike than different because all schools are measured the same way. In a standardized learning environment, the incentives to implement innovative pedagogical strategies are curtailed because the methods by which students are able to demonstrate their learning are uniform across all schools and restricted to the format of the test.

A Framework to Evaluate School Choice Policies

Levin (2002) identifies four criteria for evaluating school choice policies in a local context: freedom of choice, productive efficiency, equity, and social cohesion. These four criteria can be applied to any school choice policy to arrive at a better understanding of the underlying philosophy of a policy and the outcomes it is intended to achieve.

Freedom of choice pertains to the rights of families to choose schools for their children based on their values, individual educational philosophy, religious beliefs, and political orientation. Policies that promote freedom of choice place a greater emphasis on education as a private good and are an essential characteristic of market-based approaches to education reform such as vouchers.

Productive efficiency refers to the maximization of educational outputs. Voucher and market proponents also place considerable emphasis on productive efficiency to argue for policies that encourage deregulation and the dissolution of monopolies with the underlying purpose of maximizing the efficiency of educational service delivery in public schools.

Equity refers to the ideals of fairness in educational opportunities and outcomes. This is a universally accepted goal in US public education, which is a reason that all stakeholder groups advocate breaking the relationship between zip code and school quality. But those on both sides of the school choice debate differ in their positions about the extent to which school choice policies achieve equitable outcomes. Opponents of school choice policies, particularly those based on unregulated, market-based approaches, are concerned with the inequities associated with unfettered school choice. They point to historical evidence where poor and minority students have been shut out of quality educational opportunities and relegated to inferior, segregated schools under unregulated school choice plans. School choice opponents, however, argue that equity is achievable as the overall level of school quality rises in competitive environments.

Social cohesion pertains to the ability of public schools to provide a cohesive educational experience for all students. This common experience is foundational for a functional democracy by enabling all students to participate in the social, political, and economic institutions of society.

Those who value social cohesion as an elemental goal are more likely to view education as a public good.

Three features, or design elements, inherent in school choice plans can be manipulated to maximize the outcomes for each criterion: financing, regulation, and support services. Financing refers to the amount and allocation of funding. School choice plans, particularly those that provide per-pupil amounts for use outside the public school system, set the amount available per pupil at different levels. Friedman's school voucher approach was a low, flat amount that parents could supplement in the event that the voucher did not cover the cost of tuition. While in practice more funding is made available to cover the additional expenses associated with educating special needs students, additional funding is not available to low-income students to facilitate their participation in the program.

Regulation refers to the requirements set out by government for schools to participate in the school choice program. The question centers around the role of government in school choice. At one end, district public schools are government run, meaning that they are required to follow the rules and regulations set forth by the elected bodies that are charged with overseeing the administration of public education. Government has an influential role in the public school system. On the other end, the role of government and government regulation is limited under many school plans. Under education savings account (ESA) plans, the school program most diametrically opposed to the public school system, public dollars are provided directly to parents, who select educational providers as they see fit. There are no regulations to oversee educational service providers, government has no role in determining which providers are eligible for funding, and there are no checks on whether education providers are achieving their stated outcomes.

Support services are the publicly provided services that contribute to the functioning of the school system. These services include areas such as transportation and school-related information to inform school choice decisions. In the public education system, support services are used to remove barriers to school attendance. For example, school districts provide transportation service to students, even in remote and isolated areas. In general, support services are restricted under school choice, leaving families with the responsibility to transport their students to schools of choice. Voucher plans do not require private schools to transport participating students to school. Similarly, even in public school choice plans such as open enrollment, where students can attend a public school outside their home school district, often the receiving district public school is not required to provide transportation for students.

School-related information is a relatively new support service that has come into focus with the advancement of school choice policies. Prior to school choice, there was a limited need to provide school-related information because nearly all students attended the local neighborhood public school. In cases where students availed themselves of other school choice options, such as private schools or home schooling, these were regarded as private decisions, and the onus to acquire sufficient information to inform these decisions was on the family. Government was not obligated to provide such information.

Under school choice policies, accurate and accessible information is considered necessary to inform families as they make decisions. For this reason, school choice advocates, even market-based school choice proponents who are more likely to discourage government involvement, regard the state as the appropriate source to provide school information to inform school choice decisions. Most commonly, state governments provide information to parents through school report cards that are available to the public.

The elements of Levin's (2002) school choice framework can be combined in a myriad of ways to achieve different policy outcomes. While Friedman's voucher proposal, which emphasizes freedom of choice and efficiency, has received the most attention from policymakers, there are other voucher proposals that emphasize other criteria and different policy outcomes. For example, Jencks's (Center for the Study of Public Policy 1970) voucher proposal provided larger voucher amounts for low-income students, government regulation of student admissions, mandated standardized testing for all schools receiving vouchers, and provisions to provide transportation to participating students. Taken together, these provisions placed greater emphasis on equity and social cohesion. Jencks's proposal also required more regulation than Friedman's and dedicated resources to student support, such as transportation, to facilitate access to school choice for low-income students. A proposal by Chubb and Moe (1990) emphasizes market-based forces with limited regulations. They tempered Friedman's (1955) voucher proposals by advocating that schools of choice remain under governmental control through licensure by public entities. The licensure requirements, however, were intended to be minimalist in nature so that educational service providers would have maximum flexibility on pedagogical matters. Minimalist requirements would allow market forces, the real pistons in the education reform engine, to operate with as little friction as possible. Government licensure authority was restricted to basic requirements such as health and safety requirements and providing school performance information to parent consumers.

Looking Toward the Future of School Choice Policies

School choice will remain a prominent feature of education policy. Within the United States, the specific provisions of school choice policies will continue to evolve as more states either incorporate choice options into their education systems or modify existing school choice policies. In the international context, the successes and failures of school choice in the US context serve as a lesson for other countries looking to follow suit and institute school choice policies of their own. It is often confusing for interested citizens to assess how school choice will play out in the future amid the flurry of policy ideas, the deluge of research reports, and political bantering that, when taken together, make it difficult to follow the most important elements of education policy debates. There are three particular trends, however, that readers can follow to preview the direction that school choice policies will move in the future.

Keep an Eye on the Courts

One historical pattern for shaping education policy, including school choice, is for policymakers to use court decisions to test the boundaries of education policies. States intentionally pass school choice legislation with the expectation that the policies will be argued in the US courts. Advocates then use the wording of past court rulings to shape future school choice policies, returning to state legislatures with updated education policies that are more likely to pass constitutional challenges. This back-and-forth process is evident in the evolution of education policy from school vouchers to ESAs. For example, one key difference between school vouchers and ESAs is the direct payment to parents under ESA programs. The direct payment to parents, rather than government paying educational services, is a major reason that ESA programs circumvent Blaine amendments that prohibit state funding to education institutions with a religious affiliation. The constitutionality of this key provision has been tested in court where parental choice was used as a legal circuit breaker. Advocates used the wording from previous court decisions to craft ESA programs so that parents, not the government, make payments to educational providers, including religious schools.

Therefore, the precedents set by court decisions will be precursors to the future of school choice policies. For example, in 2017, the US Supreme Court ruled in *Trinity Lutheran Church v. Comer* that a church-run preschool could not be denied public funds to purchase rubberizing equipment for its playground through a state grant program. The church applied for the grant despite regulations that prohibit the awarding of state grants to religious institutions. In a competitive process, the church's grant application was rated high enough to receive an award, but the application was denied due to the state's constitutional ban on state aid to religious institutions. The church argued that by being denied an award that the school was otherwise qualified to receive based solely on its religious status amounted to discrimination because the church is a religious institution, violating its right to free exercise of religion. In his decision, Chief Justice John Roberts wrote that denying the church access based on its status as a religious institution "expressly discriminates against otherwise eligible recipients by disqualifying them from a public benefit solely because of their religious character" (Trinity v. Comer 2017, 2).

The US Supreme Court, in an effort to limit the reach of the decision, clarified that the ruling applied only to playground equipment. In other words, the ruling is limited because the funding was not to support a religious activity. Nevertheless, school choice proponents view the ruling as a victory because they believe that it can be applied more broadly to allow public funds to private schools for other purposes and activities. Opponents are concerned that the ruling opens the door to broader public funding to religious schools, effectively negating the separation of church and state with respect to public funding.

States Will Continue to Lead the Way

Federal policy will keep the public spotlight on school choice. President Trump's school choice plans will certainly spark conversations at all levels about school choice, and if past federal policies are an indication, it is highly likely that states may be required to implement or expand specific school choice policies as a prerequisite to receive federal funding. Yet given that the US public education system is decentralized, vesting considerable responsibility for public education in the hands of locally elected state legislators and school board members, the specifics of education policy will continue to be advanced at the state level, away from the nation's capital. Local public officials pass the bulk of education policies, and one can expect that school choice will continue to occupy a prominent place in the public discourse on how to reform public education at the state level.

States also look to other states for new ideas on school choice policies (Reznulli and Roscigno 2005). For example, given the favorable court rulings on ESAs, states looking to expand school choice policies aggressively are likely to pursue ESA programs over school vouchers. These states will watch how ESA programs play out in leading states such as Arizona, with an eye toward student participation increases, the impact of ESAs on funding for public schools, and the difficulties that may arise from virtually no accountability or regulatory requirements for education providers. States will then implement or adjust their ESA based on how these provisions function in leading states.

In addition, states policymakers often look to laws in other states for ideas to implement in their own. There are elucidative patterns with respect to the adoption of school choice policies, particularly charter school laws. Charter school laws were more likely to be adopted in states with Republican governors, particularly in states with higher percentages of students attending private schools. States with lower percentages of funding dedicated to academic instruction were also more likely to pass charter school laws in an effort to place greater emphasis on efficiency—higher academic production at a lower cost. Finally, states with longer histories of education funding litigation and higher percentages of minority students were more likely to pass charter school laws. These patterns point to a general trend where school choice policies are more likely to be adopted in states with leadership that curtails school funding and then seeks competition to reform public schools (Wong and Langevin 2006).

School Choice and Larger Societal Trends

In many ways, education policy and school choice policies reflect larger societal trends. Education will play a role to address issues such as globalization, privatization, and individualism. As a result, school choice will certainly play a role as countries and states look toward answers to these major issues, and how communities consider the role of schools to address these issues will influence the type and tenor of education policies. For example, globalization has had a transformative impact on economies, labor force requirements, and community self-identity.

In response, local communities are seeking voice in a globalized world. School choice is a way for these communities to create distinct educational options that promote their values and priorities. Similarly, as privatization takes hold in the delivery of goods and services, one can expect school choice policies to follow, particularly those forms of choice that expand educational providers to those outside government-run schools. Finally, there is a growing trend toward individualism that atomizes the scope of public policy to smaller and smaller units. Nationalistic policies encourage nations to focus inward as opposed to working on a more global scale. Similarly, the underlying premise of school choice policies is the shifting of public policy decisions to the most local unit. Under school choice policies, families are empowered to make decisions about the use of public funds, shifting policy decisions away from more collective, democratic forms of decision making.

Conclusion

If there is one overarching lesson from the school choice experiment in the United States and abroad, it's that once school choice policies begin, they have a transformative effect on public education: the number of school choice policies increases, and their scope widens. As a result, school choice policies have a profound and lasting influence on how the general public views and discusses public education. As policies evolve and diffuse, this book will be a useful resource for those who wish to understand how school choice will affect students and schools and can help shape school choice policies to improve education in their local communities.

GLOSSARY

Academic standards
Guidelines that indicate what students should know and be able to do at each grade level.

Accountability
The process of evaluating school performance based on student outcomes, namely, standardized test score results.

Blaine amendments
State constitutional provisions that prohibit state legislatures from appropriating funds to religious sects or institutions, including religious schools.

Brown v. Board of Education
A landmark US Supreme Court case that declared state laws establishing separate public schools for black and white students were unconstitutional.

Bureaucracy
An organizational structure characterized by specialization of functions, adherence to fixed rules, and a hierarchy of authority.

Charter schools
Publicly funded schools operated by independent entities. They are granted flexibility in operations and less regulation than traditional public schools in exchange for greater accountability through parental choice, along with the award and renewal of charter contracts from a governmental entity.

District public schools
Government-funded and -operated schools under the jurisdiction of locally elected governing boards and overseen by a school district.

Economies of scale
An economic principle indicating that more of a product or service produces a lower per-unit cost.

Education savings accounts (ESAs)
ESAs allow parents to withdraw their children from public district or charter schools and receive a deposit of public funds into government-authorized savings accounts to pay for educational services, including private school tuition, learning materials, and higher education expenses.

Establishment clause
A clause in the First Amendment to the US Constitution that prohibits the government from making any law "respecting an establishment of religion." The clause has been interpreted as not only forbidding the government from establishing an official religion but also prohibiting government actions that unduly favor one religion over another.

Home schooling
Home-based learning where students are educated under the supervision of their parents or legal guardians.

Local control
The degree to which local leaders, meaning those closest to the school level, make decisions about the governance and operation of public schools, and academic decisions about students.

Magnet schools
Public schools of choice that enroll students from outside established school attendance boundaries; originally created to promote desegregation.

Monopoly
One producer controls the supply of a good or service, restricting the entry of new providers.

Neighborhood public school
The public school assigned to students based on school attendance boundaries.

No Child Left Behind (NCLB)
The 2001 reauthorization of the Elementary and Secondary Education Act that expanded the federal role in public education by holding schools accountable to standardized test results.

Open enrollment
A policy that allows students to transfer to a public school of their choice. Students may be able to enroll in public schools within their school district of attendance or any public school district within their state of attendance, depending on the policy provisions.

Private schools
Autonomous schools that are supported by a private organization or individuals, to include religious institution, rather than by the government. Independent schools are a type of private school.

Public education
The institutions that collectively educate students according to public requirements.

Public school system
The collective network of public schools and their ancillary entities to include school district offices.

Racial segregation
The practice of relegating people to certain areas of residence or to separate institutions (e.g., schools, churches) on the basis of race.

School attendance boundary
Geographic boundaries that determine student assignments to public schools.

School board
Officials, most commonly elected, who direct the policies of public schools within the jurisdiction of a school district.

School district
A specific geographical area with defined boundaries that are used to organize the schools within it. Also refers to a political body established to administer public schools within the jurisdiction. In the United States, public schools are organized into school districts, which are governed by school boards.

School vouchers
A government-funded certificate redeemable for tuition fees at a private school.

Socioeconomic status (SES)
The position of persons in society based on a combination of occupational, economic, and educational criteria.

Sorting
The separation of students by academic ability; most often occurs at the school level, also referred to as "tracking."

Standardized tests
Tests that are administered and graded in the same manner to all test takers. The results or score from standardized tests are used to evaluate schools and students for accountability purposes.

Stratification
The separation of people by economic status.

Tax credits
An amount of money that taxpayers are permitted to subtract from taxes owed to their government. In education, tax credits are granted to individuals or businesses for making contributions or paying fees to a public or private school tuition organization.

White flight
The movement of white students from central cities to the suburbs to escape the influx of minorities.

OTHER RESOURCES

Brookings Institute (https://www.brookings.edu)

Center on Education Policy (https://www.cep-dc.org)

Center on Reinventing Public Education (https://www.crpe.org)

Center for Research on Education Outcomes (https://credo.stanford.edu)

Council for American Private Education (http://www.capenet.org)

Education Commission of the States (https://www.ecs.org)

Education Research Alliance for New Orleans (https://educationresearch
alliancenola.org)

Education Week (https://www.edweek.org/ew/index.html)

Friedman Foundation for Educational Change (https://www.edchoice.org)

National Alliance for Public Charter Schools (https://www.publiccharters
.org/)

National Center for Education Statistics (https://nces.ed.gov)

National Education Policy Center (http://nepc.colorado.edu)

REFERENCES

Arizona Charter School Association. n.d. About charter schools. Accessed October 9, 2017. https://azcharters.org/about-charter-schools/.

Arizona Department of Education. 2016. *Superintendent's annual report: Fiscal year 2014–2015*. Phoenix: Arizona Department of Education.

Bancroft, Kim. 2009. To have and to have not: The socioeconomics of charter schools. *Education and Urban Society* 41 (2): 248–279.

Barrows, Samuel, Paul E. Peterson, and Martin R. West. 2017. What do parents think of their children's schools? *Education Next* 17 (2).

Batdorff, Meagan, Larry Maloney, Jay F. May, Sheree T. Speakman, Patrick J. Wolf, and Albert Cheng. 2014. *Charter School Funding: Inequity Expands*. Fayetteville, AR: School Choice Demonstration Project.

Belfield, Clive R., and Henry M. Levin. 2002. The effects of competition between schools on educational outcomes: A review for the United States. *Review of Educational Research* 72 (2): 279–341.

Bell, Courtney. 2009. A choices created equal? The role of choice sets in the selection of schools. *Peabody Journal of Education* 84:191–208.

Berends, Mark, Ellen Goldring, Marc Stein, and Xiu Cravens. 2010. Instructional conditions in charter schools and students' mathematics achievement gains. *American Journal of Education* 116:303–335.

Betts, Julian, and Y. Emily Tang. 2014. A meta-analysis of the literature on the effect of charter schools on student achievement. Working paper. Seattle, WA: Center for Reinventing Public Education.

Bolick, Clint. 2017. Jump-starting K–12 education reform. *Harvard Journal of Law and Public Policy* 40 (1): 17–24.

Brandl, John E. 1985. Distilling frenzy from academic scribbling: How economics influences politicians. *Journal of Policy Analysis and Management* 4 (3): 344–353.

Brouillette, Matthew. 1999. The 1830s and 40s: Horace Mann, the end of free-market education, and the rise of government schools. Midland, MI: Mackinaw

Center for Public Policy. Accessed October 9, 2017. https://www.mackinac.org/2035.

Brown v. Board of Education of Topeka. 347 U.S. 483 (1954).

Brown, Richard W. 1968. Freedom of choice in the South: A constitutional perspective. *Louisiana Law Review* 28 (3): 455–468.

Bulkley, Katrina E. 2005. Losing voice? Educational management organizations and charter schools' educational programs. *Education and Urban Society* 37 (2): 204–234.

Burke, Lindsey. 2013. *The Education Debit Card: What Arizona Parents Purchase with Education Savings Accounts*. Washington, DC: Friedman Foundation. Accessed January 23, 2016. http://www.edchoice.org/research/the-education-debit-card/.

Callahan, Raymond E. 1962. *Education and the Cult of Efficiency*. Chicago: University of Chicago Press.

Carnoy, Martin. 2017. *School Vouchers Are Not a Proven Strategy for Improving Student Achievement*. Washington, DC: Economic Policy Institute.

Carnoy, Martin. 2000. School choice? Or is it privatization? *Educational Researcher* 29 (7): 15–20.

Carnoy, Martin, Rebecca Jacobsen, Lawrence Mishel, and Richard Rothstein. 2005. *The Charter School Dust Up: Examining the Evidence on Enrollment and Achievement*. New York: Teachers College Press.

Carruthers, Celeste K. 2012. New schools, new students, new teachers: Evaluating the effectiveness of charter schools. *Economics of Education Review* 31:280–292.

Center for Research on Education Outcomes. 2013. *National Charter School Study 2013*. Stanford, CA: Center for Research on Education Outcomes.

Center for Research on Education Outcomes. 2015. *Online Charter School Study 2015*. Stanford, CA: Center for Research on Education Outcomes.

Center for Research on Education Outcomes. 2017a. *Charter Management Organizations 2017*. Stanford, CA: Center for Research on Education Outcomes.

Center for Research on Education Outcomes. 2017b. *Charter Schools: Quality Educational Options that Improve All Schools*. Washington, DC: Center for Research on Education Outcomes.

Center for the Study of Public Policy. 1970. *Educational Vouchers. Report Prepared for the U.S. Office of Economic Opportunity.* Cambridge, MA: Center for the Study of Public Policy.

Center on Education Policy. 2007. *Are Private High Schools Better Academically Than Public High Schools?* Washington, DC: Center on Education Policy.

Cheng, Albert, Collin Hitt, Brian Kisida, and Jonathan N. Mills. 2017. No excuses charter schools: A meta-analysis of the experimental evidence on student achievement. *Journal of School Choice* 11 (2): 209–238.

Chingos, Matthew M., and Paul P. Peterson. 2013. The impact of school vouchers on college enrollment. *Education Next* 13 (3). Accessed January 19, 2018. http://educationnext.org/the-impact-of-school-vouchers-on-college-enrollment/.

Chubb, J., and Terry M. Moe. 1990. *Politics, Markets and America's Schools.* Washington, DC: Brookings Institution.

Cobb, Casey D., and Gene V. Glass. 1999. Ethnic segregation in Arizona charter schools. *Education Policy Analysis Archives* 7. Accessed January 17, 2018. https://epaa.asu.edu/ojs/article/view/536.

Council for American Private Education. 2017. *FAQs About Private Schools.* Accessed August 3, 2017. http://www.capenet.org/facts.html.

Center for Education Reform. 2014. *Survey of America's Charter Schools.* Accessed September 10, 2017. https://www.edreform.com/wp-content/uploads/2014/02/2014CharterSchoolSurveyFINAL.pdf.

Edchoice. n.d. The ABC's of school choice. Accessed October 10, 2017. https://www.edchoice.org/research/the-abcs-of-school-choice/.

Education Commission of the States. 2016a. Open Enrollment: 50-State Report. Accessed July 28, 2017. http://ecs.force.com/mbdata/mbquest4e?rep=OE1605.

Education Commission of the States. 2016b. Charter schools—How is the funding for a charter school determined? Accessed October 7, 2017. http://ecs.force.com/mbdata/mbquestNB2?rep=CS1521.

Elacqua, Gregory, Mark Schneider, and Jack Buckley. 2006. School choice in Chile: Is it class or classroom? *Journal of Policy Analysis and Management* 25 (3): 577–601.

Epple, Dennis, Richard E. Romano, and Miguel Urquiola. 2017. School vouchers: A survey of the economics literature. *Journal of Economic Literature* 55 (2): 441–492.

Fava, Eileen M. 1991. Desegregation and parental choice in public schooling: A legal analysis of controlled choice student assignment plans. *Boston College Third World Law Journal* 11 (1): 83–104.

Finn, Chester E., Jr., Bruno V. Manno, and Gregg Vanourek. 2000. *Charter Schools in Action: Renewing Public Education*. Princeton, NJ: Princeton University Press.

Finnigan, Kara S. 2007. Charter school autonomy: The mismatch between theory and practice. *Educational Policy* 21 (3): 503–526.

Fiske, Edward B., and Helen F. Ladd. 2000. *When Schools Compete: A Cautionary Tale*. Washington, DC: Brookings Institution Press.

Forster, Greg. 2016. *A Win-Win Solution: The Empirical Evidence on School Choice*. Indianapolis, IN: Friedman Foundation for Educational Choice.

Frankenberg, Erica, Genevieve Seigel-Hawley, and Jia Wang. 2010. *Choice without Equity: Charter School Standards and the Need for Civil Rights Standards*. Los Angeles: The Civil Rights Project.

Friedman, Milton. 1955. The role of government in education. In *Economics and the Public Interest*, edited by R. A. Solo, 123–144. New Brunswick, NJ: Rutgers University Press.

Fuller, Bruce, ed. 2000. *Inside Charter Schools: The Paradox of Radical Decentralization*. Cambridge, MA: Harvard University Press.

Fusarelli, Lance D. 2001. The political construction of accountability: When rhetoric meets reality. *Education and Urban Society* 33 (2): 157–169.

Fyer, Roland G. 2014. Injecting charter school best practices into traditional public schools: Evidence from field experiments. *Quarterly Journal of Economics* 129 (3): 1355–1407.

Garcia, Amaya. 2017. Chile's school voucher system: Enabling choice or perpetuating social inequality? *New America*, February 9. Accessed August 5, 2017. https://www.newamerica.org/education-policy/edcentral/chiles-school -voucher-system-enabling-choice-or-perpetuating-social-inequality/.

Garcia, David R. 2008. The impact of school choice on racial segregation in charter schools. *Educational Policy* 22 (6): 805–829.

Garcia, David R. 2012. Protecting the choice to stay: Education savings accounts and legislative priorities. *Teachers College Record*, December 7.

Garcia, David R., Lee McIlroy, and Rebecca T. Barber. 2008. Starting behind: A comparative analysis of the academic standing of students entering charter schools. *Social Science Quarterly* 89 (1): 199–216.

Giles, Corrie, and Andrew Hargreaves. 2006. The sustainability of innovative schools as learning organizations and professional learning communities during standardized reform. *Educational Administration Quarterly* 42 (1): 124–156.

Green v. County School Board of New Kent County. 391 U.S. 430 (1968).

Griffin, Noelle C., and Priscilla Wohlstetter. 2001. Building a plane while flying it: Early lessons from developing charter schools. *Teachers College Record* 103 (2): 336–365.

Harris, Douglas N. 2017. *Why Managed Competition Is Better Than a Free Market for Schooling.* Washington, DC: Brookings Institute. Accessed September 21, 2017. https://www.brookings.edu/opinions/why-managed-competition-is-better-than-a-free-market-for-schooling/.

Harris, Douglas N., and Matthew Larsen. 2016. *The Effects of the New Orleans Post-Katrina School Reforms on Student Academic Outcomes.* New Orleans: Education Research Alliance for New Orleans.

Henig, Jeffrey. 1994. *Rethinking School Choice: Limits of the Market Metaphor.* Princeton, NJ: Princeton University Press.

Henig, Jeffrey R. 2008. *Spin Cycle: How Research Is Used in Policy Debates: The Case of Charter Schools.* New York: Russell Sage Foundation.

Henig, Jeffrey R. 2009. Politicization of evidence: Lessons for an informed democracy. *Educational Policy* 23 (1): 137–160.

Hess, Frederick. 2001. Whaddya mean you want to close my school? The politics of regulatory accountability in charter schooling. *Education and Urban Society* 33 (2): 141–156.

Hill, Paul T., Robin J. Lake, Mary Beth Celio, Christine Campbell, Paul A. Herdman, and Katrina E. Bulkley. 2001. *Charter School Accountability: National Charter School Accountability Study.* Seattle: Center on Reinventing Public Education.

Howard, Philip K. 2012. To fix America's education bureaucracy, we need to destroy it. *Atlantic*, April 2. Accessed October 2, 2017. https://www.theatlantic.com/national/archive/2012/04/to-fix-americas-education-bureaucracy-we-need-to-destroy-it/255173/

Hoxby, Caroline M. 2001. School choice and school productivity: Could school choice be a tide that lifts all boats? In *The Economics of School Choice*, edited by Caroline Hoxby. Chicago: University of Chicago Press.

Hoxby, Caroline M., Sonali Murarka, and Jenny Kang. 2009. How New York City's charter schools affect achievement. In *The New York City Charter Schools Evaluation*. Stanford: New York City Charter Schools Evaluation Project.

Institute for Justice. 2017. Answers to frequently asked questions about Blaine amendments. Accessed October 7, 2017. http://ij.org/issues/school-choice/blaine-amendments/answers-frequently-asked-questions-blaine-amendments/.

Jeynes, William H. 2012. A meta-analysis on the effects and contributions of public, public charter, and religious schools on student outcomes. *Peabody Journal of Education* 87 (3): 305–335.

Katz, Michael S. 1976. *A History of Compulsory Education Laws*. Bloomington, IN: Phi Delta Kappan.

Kimbrough, Ralph B., and Eugene A. Todd. 1967. Bureaucratic organization. *Educational Leadership* (December): 220–224.

Klein, Naomi. 2008. *The Shock Doctrine: The Rise of Disaster Capitalism*. New York: Picador.

Kolderie, Ted. 1990. *Beyond Choice to New Public Schools: Withdrawing the Exclusive Franchise in Public Education*. Washington, DC: Progressive Policy Institute.

Lacireno-Paquet, Natalie, Thomas T. Holyoke, Michelle Moser, and Jeffrey R. Henig. 2002. Creaming versus cropping: Charter school enrollment practices in response to market incentives. *Educational Evaluation and Policy Analysis* 24 (2): 145–158.

Ladd, Helen F., and Edward B. Fiske. 2001. The uneven playing field of school choice: Evidence from New Zealand. *Journal of Policy Analysis and Management* 20 (1): 43–64.

Ladner, Matthew. 2012. *The Way of the Future: Education Savings Accounts for Every American Family.* Indianapolis, IN: Friedman Foundation. Accessed December 29, 2017. http://www.edchoice.org/research/the-way-of-the-future/.

Lake, Robin J. 2008. In the eye of the beholder: Charter schools and innovation. *Journal of School Choice* 2 (2): 115–127.

Lantta, Luke A. 2004. The post-Zelman voucher battleground: Where to turn after federal Blaine amendments fail. *Law and Contemporary Problems* 67:213–242.

Lee, Jaekyung. 2002. Racial and ethnic achievement gap trends: Reversing the progress toward equity? *Educational Researcher* 31 (1): 3–12.

Levin, Henry M. 2002. A comprehensive framework for evaluating educational vouchers. *Educational Evaluation and Policy Analysis* 24 (3): 159–174.

Lubienski, Christopher. 2001. Redefining public education: Charter schools, common schools and the rhetoric of reform. *Teachers College Record* 103 (4): 634–666.

Lubienski, Christopher. 2003. Innovation in education markets: Theory and evidence on the impact of competition and choice in charter schools. *American Educational Research Journal* 40 (2): 395–443.

Lubienski, Christopher. 2007. Marketing schools: Consumer goods and competitive incentives for consumer information. *Education and Urban Society* 40 (1): 118–141.

Lubienski, Christopher L., and Sara T. Lubienski. 2014. *The Public School Advantage: Why Public Schools Outperform Private Schools.* Chicago: University of Chicago Press.

Macey, Erin, Janet Decker, and Suzanne E. Eckes. 2009. The Knowledge Is Power Program (KIPP): An analysis of one model's efforts to promote achievement in underserved communities. *Journal of School Choice* 3 (3): 212–241.

Manno, Bruno V., Chester E. Finn, Jr., Louann A. Bierlein, and Gregg Vanourek. 1998. Charter schools: Accomplishments and dilemmas. *Teachers College Record* 99 (3): 537–558.

Maranto, Robert, Scott Milliman, Frederick Hess, and April Grisham, eds. 1999. *School Choice in the Real World: Lessons from Arizona Charter Schools.* Boulder, CO: Westview Press.

McEwan, Patrick J. 2000. The potential impact of large-scale voucher programs. *Review of Educational Research* 70 (2): 103–149.

McNeil, Linda. 2000. *Contradictions of School Reform: Costs of Standardized Testing*. New York: Routledge.

Mead, Julie F. 2015. The right to an education or the right to shop for schooling: Examining voucher programs in relation to state constitutional guarantees. *Fordham Urban Law Journal* 42:703–743.

Mead, Julie F., and Maria M. Lewis. 2016. The implications of the use of parental choice as a legal circuit breaker. *American Educational Research Journal* 53 (1): 100–131.

Mills, Jonathan N., and Patrick J. Wolf. 2016. The effects of the Louisiana Scholarship Program on student achievement after two years. School Choice Demonstration Project. Accessed on October 8, 2017. https://educationresearch alliancenola.org/files/publications/Report-1-LSP-Y2-Achievement.pdf.

Murrell, Peter C. 1999. Chartering the village: The making of an African-centered charter school. *Urban Education* 33 (5): 565–583.

Nathan, Joe. 1996. *Charter Schools: Creating Hope and Opportunity for American Education*. San Francisco: Jossey-Bass.

National Alliance for Public Charter Schools. 2017a. Charter School Data Dashboard. Accessed October 6, 2017. http://www.publiccharters.org.

National Alliance for Public Charter Schools. 2017b. Measuring up to the model: A ranking of state charter public school laws. Accessed October 6, 2017. http://www.publiccharters.org/publications/measuring-model-ranking-state -charter-public-school-laws/

National Association for the Advancement of Colored People. 2016. Statement regarding the NAAACP's resolution on a moratorium on charter schools. October 15. Accessed October 8, 2017. http://www.naacp.org/latest/ statement-regarding-naacps-resolution-moratorium-charter-schools/.

National Center for Education Statistics. 2015. *Digest of Education Statistics*. Accessed October 8, 2017. https://nces.ed.gov/programs/digest/.

National Center for Education Statistics. 2017a. Characteristics of Private Schools in the United States: Results from the 2015–2016 Private School

Universe Survey. Accessed January 15, 2018 at https://nces.ed.gov/pubs2017/2017073.pdf.

National Center for Education Statistics. 2017b. Characteristics of Traditional Public Schools and Public Charter Schools. Accessed October 8, 2017. https://nces.ed.gov/programs/coe/indicator_cla.asp.

National Center for Education Statistics. 2017c. [Public Charter School Enrollment.] *Condition of Education* 2017:2017–2144.

Ni, Yongmei. 2009. The impact of charter schools on the efficiency of traditional public schools: Evidence from Michigan. *Economics of Education Review* 28:571–584.

Niehaus v. Huppenthal. Maricopa County Superior Court of Arizona. 310 P.3d 983 (2013).

Opfer, V. Darleen. 2001. Charter schools and the panoptic effect of accountability. *Education and Urban Society* 33 (2): 201–215.

Orfield, Gary, Erica Frankenberg, Jongyeon Ee, and John Kuscera. 2014. *Brown at 60 Great Progress, a Long Retreat and an Uncertain Future.* Los Angeles: Civil Rights Project.

Peterson, Paul E., Michael B. Henderson, Martin R. West, and Samuel Barrows. 2017. Ten years in public opinion from the EdNext poll. *Education Next* 17 (1).

Petrilli, Michael J. 2005. Charters as role models. *Education Next* 5 (3): 56–58.

Portales, Jaime, and Julian V. Heilig. 2014. Understanding how universal vouchers have impacted urban school districts' enrollment in Chile. *Education Policy Analysis Archives* 22 (72): 1–39.

Prothero, Arianna. 2018. Homeschooling: Requirements, research and who does it. *Education Week*, January 10.

Ravitch, Diane. 2010. *The Death and Life of the Great American School System: How Testing and Choice Are Undermining Education.* New York: Basic Books.

Reardon, Sean F., and John T. Yun. 2002. *Private School Racial Enrollments and Segregation.* Cambridge, MA: Civil Rights Project, Harvard University.

Religious Action Center of Reform Judaism. 2017. Jewish values and school vouchers. Accessed December 29, 2017. https://rac.org/jewish-values-and-school-vouchers.

Renzulli, Linda A., and Lorraine Evans. 2005. School choice, charter schools, and white flight. *Social Problems* 52 (3): 398–418.

Renzulli, Linda A., and Vincent J. Roscigno. 2005. Charter school policy, implementation, and diffusion across the United States. *Sociology of Education* 78 (4): 344–365.

Roda, Allison, and Amy S. Wells. 2013. School choice policies and racial segregation: Where white parents' good intentions, anxiety, and privilege collide. *American Journal of Education* 119 (2): 261–293.

Rofes, Eric. 1998. *How Are School Districts Responding to Charter Laws and Charter Schools? A Study of Eight States and the District of Columbia.* Berkeley: Policy Analysis for California Education.

Rofes, E., and Lisa M. Stulberg, eds. 2004. *The Emancipatory Promise of Charter Schools: Towards a Progressive Politics of School Choice.* Albany: SUNY Press.

Rose, Lowell C., and Alec M. Gallup. 2002. Responsible polling. *Education Next* 2: 3.

Sass, Tim R. 2006. Charter schools and student achievement in Florida. *Education Finance and Policy* 1:91–122.

Schnaiberg, Lynn. 1998. Predominantly black charters focus of debate in N.C. *Education Week*, August 5, 22.

Schneider, Mark, and Jack Buckley. 2002. What do parents want from schools? Evidence from the Internet. *Educational Evaluation and Policy Analysis* 24 (2): 133–144.

Shanker, Albert. 1988. National Press Club speech, March 31. Accessed October 8, 2017. http://reuther.wayne.edu/files/64.43.pdf.

Shober, Arnold F., and Michael T. Hartney. 2014. *Does School Board Leadership Matter?* Washington, DC: Thomas B. Fordham Foundation.

Sirin, Selcuk R. (2005). Socioeconomic status and academic achievement: A meta-analytic review of research. *Review of Educational Research* 75 (3): 417–453.

Smith, Adam. 2000. *The Wealth of Nations/Adam Smith: Introduction by Robert Reich; edited, with notes, marginal summary, and enlarged index by Edwin Cannan, 1723–1790* . New York: Modern Library.

Southern Education Foundation. 2016. *Race and Ethnicity in a New Era of Public Funding of Private Schools: Private School Enrollment in the South and the Nation.* Atlanta, GA: Author.

SRI International. 2002. *A Decade of Public Charter Schools: Evaluation of the Public Charter Schools Program: 2000–2001 Evaluation Report.* Washington, DC: Author.

Strauss, Valerie. 2017. Do traditional public schools benefit from charter competition? *Washington Post*, August 28, https://www.washingtonpost.com/news/answer-sheet/wp/2017/08/28/do-traditional-public-schools-benefit-from-charter-competition/.

Stulberg, Lisa M. 2006. School choice discourse and the legacy of *Brown*. *Journal of School Choice* 1 (1): 23–45.

Teske, Paul, Mark Schneider, Jack Buckley, and Sarah Clark. 2000. *Does Charter School Competition Improve Traditional Public Schools?* New York: Manhattan Institute.

Thelin, Mikael, and Thomas Niedomysl. 2015. The (ir)relevance of geography for school choice: Evidence from a Swedish choice experiment. *Geoforum* 67:110–120.

Trinity Lutheran Church of Columbia v. Comer. 137 S. Ct: 2012, 198 L. Ed. Zd 551 (2017).

Trump, Donald J. 2017. Remarks by President Trump in joint address to Congress. Accessed January 4, 2018. https://www.whitehouse.gov/the-press-office/2017/02/28/remarks-president-trump-joint-address-congress.

Tyack, David B. 1974. *The One Best System: A History of American Urban Education.* Cambridge, MA: Harvard University Press.

Tyack, David B., and Larry Cuban. 1995. *Tinkering Toward Utopia: A Century of Public School Reform.* Cambridge, MA: Harvard University Press.

US Census Bureau. 2015. *Public Education Finances: 2013.* Washington, DC: US Census Bureau.

US Department of Education. 2000. *Evaluation of the Public Charter Schools Program: Year One Evaluation Report.* Washington, DC: US Department of Education.

US Department of Education. 2001. Executive summary: Press release. January. Accessed October 8, 2017. https://www2.ed.gov/nclb/overview/intro/execsumm.html.

US Department of Education. 2009. Executive summary: Race to the Top program. November. Accessed January 8, 2018. https://www2.ed.gov/programs/racetothetop/executive-summary.pdf.

US News and World Report. 2017. Best high schools. Accessed October 9, 2017. https://www.usnews.com/education/best-high-schools.

Weiher, Gregory R., and Kent L. Tedin. 2002. Does choice lead to racially distinctive schools? Charter schools and household preferences. *Journal of Policy Analysis and Management* 21 (1): 79–92.

Weixler, Lindsay B., Nathan Barrett, and Jennifer Jennings. 2017. *Did the New Orleans School Reforms Increase Segregation?* New Orleans: Education Research Alliance for New Orleans.

Welner, Kevin. 2008. *NeoVouchers: The Emergence of Tuition Tax Credits for Private Schools*. Lanham, MD: Rowman & Littlefield.

Welner, Kevin. 2017. Tax credits, school choice and "neo-vouchers": What you need to know. *The Conversation*, April 14. Accessed January 8, 2018. http://theconversation.com/tax-credits-school-choice-and-neovouchers-what-you-need-to-know-74808.

West, Martin R., Michael B. Henderson, Paul P. Peterson, and Samuel Barrows. 2018. The 2017 EdNext poll on school reform. *Education Next* 18 (1).

Wolf, Patrick J. 2012. The Comprehensive Longitudinal Evaluation of the Milwaukee Parental Choice Program: Summary of final reports. Fayetteville, AR: School Choice Demonstration Project.

Wolf, Patrick, Brian Kisida, Babette Gutmann, Michael Puma, Nada Eissa, and Lou Rizzo. 2013. School vouchers and student outcomes: Experimental evidence from Washington, DC. *Journal of Policy Analysis and Management* 32 (2): 246–270.

Wong, Kenneth K., and Warren E. Langevin. 2006. *Policy Expansion of School Choice in the American States*. Nashville, TN: National Center on School Choice.

Wong, Manyee, Thomas D. Cook, and Peter M. Steiner. 2015. Adding design elements to improve time series designs: No Child Left Behind as an example of causal pattern-matching. *Journal of Research on Educational Effectiveness* 8 (2): 245–279.

Yancey, Patty. 2004. Independent black schools and the charter movement. In *The Emancipatory Promise of Charter Schools*, ed. Eric Rofes and Lisa M. Stulberg. Albany, NY: SUNY Press.

Yeh, Stuart S. 2013. A re-analysis of the effects of KIPP and the Harlem Promise Academies. *Teachers College Record* 115:1–20.

Zelman v. Simmons-Harris. 536 U.S. 639 (2002).

Zimmer, Ron, and Cassandra M. Guarino. 2013. Is there empirical evidence that charter schools push out low-performing students? *Educational Evaluation and Policy Analysis* 35 (4): 461–480.

INDEX

DAVID R. GARCIA is Associate Professor in the Mary Lou Fulton Teachers College at Arizona State University. Prior to ASU, he served as the Associate Superintendent of Public Instruction for the state of Arizona, as a research analyst for the Arizona state legislature and as a national peer consultant. He works with many community organizations on education policy issues. His academic publications focus on school choice, accountability, and the factors that facilitate or distort policy implementation in public education. His research has appeared in numerous journals including *Teachers College Record*, *Educational Policy*, and the *Journal of School Choice*. In addition, he was coeditor of *Review of Research in Education* and an associate editor for *Education Policy Analysis*, leading academic journals in education. In 2008, he was awarded the National Academy of Education/Spencer Postdoctoral Fellowship. In 2015 and 2016, he was recognized nationally as an influential public scholar according to the edu-scholar rankings. Garcia received a Bachelor of Arts and Honors Diploma from Arizona State University. He also holds a Master of Arts and Doctor of Philosophy from the University of Chicago in Education Policy, Research and Institutional Studies.